Devotion
to the Saints

by

Anna Riva

Author of

Prayer Book
Power of the Psalms
Candle Burning Magic
Devotions to The Saints
Secrets of Magical Seals
The Modern Herbal Spellbook
Modern Witchcraft Spellbook
Golden Secrets of Mystic Oils
Magic With Incense and Powders
Spellcraft, Hexcraft & Witchcraft
Voodoo Handbook of Cult Secrets
Your Lucky Number ... Forever
How to Conduct a Seance

INTERNATIONAL IMPORTS
236 W. MANCHESTER AVE,
LOS ANGELES, CA 90003
www.indloproducts.com

Copyright © 1984
Reprint 2007

Occult Books · Curios · Supplies   ISBN 0-9438-3208-X

CONTENTS

But thou, when thou prayest, enter into thy closet, and when thou hast shut the door, pray to thy Father which is in secret: and thy Father which seeth in secret shall reward thee openly.

Matthew 6:6

INTRODUCTION

Why another book on the saints? Because this one hopes to offer an approach not taken by other authors. This volume will give you a brief sketch of their lives so that their personal circumstances and their triumphs over temptations and tribulations may prove an inspiration to the reader. Also, an attempt has been made to present the information neglected in other books about the saints . . . which saints can be asked to intercede for various health conditions, the patron saints of your job so that you can get help when needed, and the special aid certain saints can offer for those particular situations or those specific problems we all encounter from time to time. So, in brief, this is a book to read and to use—everyday, or whenever an occasion arises that guidance, comfort, assistance, or inspiration is needed.

What is a saint? According to a dictionary, a saint is a person recognized by the Church as having, by holiness of life and heroic virtue, attained a high place in heaven and, therefore, entitled to the devotion of the faithful, fit to serve as a spiritual model, and able to intercede for others in the courts of God. Saints were not angels on earth, but were human beings, with faults and failures, with weaknesses and sins. There were war-mongering saints, and pacifists. They lost their tempers, made mistakes, and regretted them. Only love of God made them unique. For it they would forsake the world, give up their possessions, and subdue their desires in favor of service to others. They found riches in poverty, happiness in sorrow, and joy in pain.

There is an astounding variety and wonderful diversity between their lives. There were kings and queens and those of shoddy, poor, or humble backgrounds. Saints of giant intellect, and saints who lacked scholarship. Gentlemen and ruffians, those who roamed the world and those who never ventured more than a few miles from home. Some lived riotously, fought recklessly, and loved lustily before their conversion. Some died in childhood and some lived well over a century. Saints are white, brown, yellow, black. No country has not bred those who seem to have been possessed by God. Their only common bond seems to be that they were love-struck, God-struck.

What makes a person a saint? One answer is this simple but significant explanation, and could serve us all as our aim in life.

"They were cheerful when it was difficult to be cheerful.
Patient when it was difficult to be patient.
Because they pushed on, when they wanted to stand still;
They kept silent, when they wanted to talk,
They were agreeable, when they wanted to be disagreeable.
That was all. It was quite simple."

These people became saints because of the sustained goodness of their lives, or, because in earlier centuries, they died a martyr's death for their Christian faith. This led them to become popular heroes as well as shining examples by whose reflected light lesser men and women might steer their own difficult lives. By the end of the second century, the anniversaries of their deaths were beginning to be celebrated as days of joy and pious observance. The tombs that contained their bones were "more precious than precious stones and finer than gold" as an ancient writer described them.

Because the saints lived in the hearts of the people, and became regarded as patrons and protectors, it was inevitable that legends of all kinds would gather round their names. Real incidents were embroidered and enlarged by enthusiastic storytellers. Gaps in their history were filled in with details which may have been probable or suitable, but not necessarily complete and unconditional truth. The fewer known facts available, the wider the field for the imagination, and floating folk tales were often added to the traditions. Thus by written word and oral history the great saints of the early years entered into the folklore for compliers were anxious to glorify their heroes.

Can prayers to the saints help us in our personal lives? There are many Biblical references which bid us to venerate the angels. Matthew 18: Verse 10 says, "... I say to you, That in heaven their angels do always behold the face of my Father ..." And Exodus 23: Verse 20, "Behold, I send an angel before thee, to keep thee in the way, and to bring thee into the place which I have prepared." Also, Psalms 91: Verses 11 and 12, "For he shall give his angels charge over thee, to keep thee in all thy ways. They shall bear thee up in their hands, lest thou dash thy foot against a stone." If St. Paul beseeches his brethren to help him by their prayers for him to God, we can with even greater reason maintain that we can be helped by the prayers of the saints, and ask for their intercession with humility. If we ask our relatives and friends on earth to join us in our devotions and petitions, why not those who live in heaven with God?

There has been no attempt to make this book complete or absolutely factual. Completeness would be impossible, for one source alone lists over five thousand saints. There are two hundred nineteen Saint Johns, one hundred twenty three Saint Peters, and more than fifty each of Saints Felix, Thomas, Paul, and Francis. The biographical information and the dates of the saint's life are as factual as possible, but many birth and death dates are obscure and the material about their lives is, particularly in regard to earlier saints, largely legendary.

The Feast Day is the commemoration of the day of the saint's death. This is true for all except Saint John the Baptist whose feast day is June 24, his birthday. There is another on August 29, the day of his death, but the primary Feast of St. John the Baptist is June 24.

Does everyone have a personal saint? You certainly do if you want one! In Roman Catholic baptism or confirmation rites, a patron saint is chosen, usually one with the same or similar name to your own. But this is not necessary. One can choose any saint and, after reading the short biographies, there may be one whose life, trials, or virtues seem to have special appeal. If so, then by all means be guided by these attributes rather than the name. And, should a particular saint inspire you to learn more about them, there are many full length biographies of saints available in your library or book store.

Once a personal patron saint is chosen, go to them as you would a friend. Join with them in spirit, as you would with an earthly friend in person, and share with them your joys, your problems, your failures, your triumphs. There can only be gain in spiritual growth by accepting a saint as your personal guide and confidant.

An exclusive feature of this book are the indexes which give hundreds of objectives, purposes, situations, problems, and work or health conditions, where the saints may be able to assist, relieve, improve, refresh, console, or enrich your life.

There are many prayers scattered throughout the book, and an entire section of devotions for various purposes. Use them freely, or compose your own. It is the author's prayer and sincere belief that your life will become blessed with more blessings than ever dreamed of.

ANNA RIVA

November, 1982

Meeting of St. Francis and St. Dominic

LIVES OF THE SAINTS

ST. ACACIUS (3rd century)   **MAY 8**

An officer in the Roman army, he became a Christian, along with his nine thousand men, just before a battle. They won the battle, but he and his men were arrested for their faith. They were tortured, but then they converted their one thousand executioners. More executioners were summoned. Acacius and his ten thousand men had crowns of thorns placed on their heads and were then crucified.

† † † † † † † † †

ST. AGATHA (3rd century)   **FEBRUARY 5**

Although Agatha's martyrdom is authenticated, there is little reliable information about her life or details of her death. According to later records, she was the daughter of a distinguished Sicilian family and remarkable for her outstanding beauty. After rejecting the advances of the Roman governor, Quintianus, he had her subjected to various cruel tortures. Her breasts were cut off with a pair of scissors, she was rolled on pieces of broken pottery, then on burning coals. None of these killed her so she was returned to her cell while the stake was prepared. She died praying before the fires were ready for her burning.

A year after her death, the city was menaced by an eruption of Mount Etna. A silk veil was taken from Agatha's tomb and flown. This caused the volcano to quiet and the molten streams stopped before destroying the city.

† † † † † † † † †

ST. AGIA (7th century)   **APRIL 18**

She was wife of Hidulf, but they separated because both wanted to enter the religious life. She entered a nunnery and he became a monk.

For reasons unknown, Agia is called upon to help in lawsuits.

† † † † † † † † †

ST. ALBERT (1205 - 1280)   **NOVEMBER 15**

Born at Lauingen, a small town in Bavaria, Albertus Magnus was the oldest son of a powerful lord, the Count of Bollstadt. Albert is called "the wonder and the miracle of his age" in recognition of his extraordinary genius and extensive knowledge. His life was spent studying, teaching, and writing. A teacher of St. Thomas Aquinas, he became one of the most highly honored professors at the University of Paris. Author of thirty eight volumes, including treatises on logic, metaphysics, ethics, physics, geography, biology, mineralogy, astronomy, botany, animal physiology, and the experimental sciences as well as biblical and theological works. Albert gathered into one vast encyclopedia all that was known in his day, and then expressed his own opinions. His zeal was always tempered with patience and charity, and the belief that faith and science must go hand in hand. It can be from him that the secret of combining human wisdom and knowledge with divine trust and assurance may be learned.

† † † † † † † † †

ST. ALOYSIUS GONZAGA (1568 - 1591)   JUNE 21

The son of a high ranking official in the Spanish court, Aloysius' father had him train as a very small boy with miniature guns and march at the head of a platoon in a military parade, but by the age of nine Aloysius had decided on a career of service to the church and to others. Finally, at the age of seventeen, he secured his father's permission to study for the priesthood. In 1591, when he was in his fourth year of theology studies, an epidemic of plague broke out in Italy. Even though he was in delicate health, he devoted himself to the care of the victims. He himself was struck down by the disease and died at the age of twenty three.

† † † † † † † † †

ST. AMBROSE (340 - 397)   DECEMBER 7

St. Ambrose was the youngest child of a high official of Gaul who ruled the territories which are now France, Britain, Spain, and part of Africa. Two older children, his brother Satyrus and sister Marcellina, are also saints. His mother was a teacher, who assisted in the early religious training of the children and encouraged his secular education.

He became a lawyer, writer, outstanding preacher and pastor, beloved bishop, and a protector of the poor. It was he who converted and baptized St. Augustine. As a preacher, one of his favorite topics was the excellence of virginity, and was so successful in persuading the maidens at his services that many mothers refused to allow their daughters to listen to his words. Ambrose refuted the charge that he was trying to depopulate the world by quaintly inquiring of young men if they had experienced any difficulty in finding wives.

His daily life was filled with throngs of visitors—high officials seeking advice on affairs of state and repentent sinners seeking absolution for personal sins. He ate sparingly, dining only on Saturdays, Sundays, and festivals of the more celebrated martyrs. He spent long hours in prayer, attended to his vast correspondence, wrote many books, and read profusely. His indefatigable energy and his methodical habits explain how he managed to produce such an immense volume of work and, at the same time, attend to his bodily, spiritual, and social requirments. It would be well to remember that much can be accomplished when dedication, enthusiasm, and discipline are used to bring order into what may seem to be chaotic conditions.

Below is an example of his poetry.

"No sinful word, nor deed of wrong,
Nor thoughts that idly rove;
But simple truth be on our tongue,
And in our hearts be love."

ST. AMBROSE'S PRAYER
O Lord, who has mercy upon all,
take away from me my sins,
and mercifully kindle in me the fire of Thy Holy Spirit.
Take away from me the heart of stone,
and give me a heart of flesh,
a heart to love and adore Thee,
a heart to delight in Thee,
to follow and to enjoy Thee, for Christ's sake.

† † † † † † † † †

ST. ANDREW the Apostle (1st century)   NOVEMBER 30

Andrew was a fisherman, a disciple of John the Baptist, the elder brother of St. Peter, and the first to be called to be Christ's disciple. He brought Peter, whose name at that time was Simon, to Jesus and he also joined the group who would be the messengers of the messiah's coming. It was Andrew who, according to John VI,

Verses 8 and 9, called to Jesus' attention, "There is a lad here, which hath five barley loaves, and two small fishes, but what are they among so many?" And from these, Jesus fed the five thousand who had come to hear him speak.

Little is known of his later life, but Andrew is believed to have been the first to preach in Poland and in Russia. It is generally agreed that he died on November 30, AD 60, during the reign of Nero. He was bound, not nailed to the cross, in order to prolong his sufferings, and the cross was shaped like an X, the decussate cross, now known as St. Andrew's cross.

† † † † † † † † †

ST. ANDREW AVELLINO (1521 - 1608)   NOVEMBER 10

Christened Lancelot when he was born near Naples, Italy, he changed his name to Andrew when he entered the religious life. He was a handsome youth, much devoted to chastity, and when he felt threatened by young female admirers, he had the crown of his head shaved as a declaration of his commitment to sexual abstinence.

Personally he was truly humble and sincerely pious, and he had a fervent zeal for strict religious discipline. His time was spent writing, preaching, hearing confessions, and visiting the sick. At the age of eighty eight he died of a seizure at the foot of the altar at the beginning of services.

† † † † † † † † †

ST. ANNE (1st century)   JULY 26

Though the parents of the Blessed Virgin Mary are not mentioned in the Bible, tradition gives them as Joachim, a rich farmer, and his wife, Anne, or Hannah. Since Anne was past the child bearing years when Mary was born, it is believed that she was miraculously conceived, as Jesus was conceived later by Mary.

Some writers say that Anne taught her small daughter to read scripture. Others believe that at the age of three, Mary was taken to the Temple where she lived among the virgins.

Many faithful believe that those who devoutly say prayers in honor of St. Anne on Tuesday of any week are granted numerous favors.

PRAYER FOR BLESSINGS

With a sincere heart, I kneel before thee, O glorious Saint Anne. Thou art blessed with extraordinary virtues and holiness and did merit from God the high favor of giving life to Blessed Mary, Mother of God.

Grant that I may know my sins and weep over them in bitterness of heart. Save me from every danger that confronts me in life, and help me at the hour of death. Obtain for me from God the power to imitate those virtues with which thou wast adorned.

PRAYER FOR TRANQUILITY

Give me this day, Saint Anne, the grace and strength to forbear and to persevere. Grant me courage and a quiet mind. May I be brave in peril, constant in tribulation, temperate in wrath, and serene in all changes of fortune. Let me be loyal and loving to all those who touch my life today.

† † † † † † † † †

ST. ANTHONY the Great (251 - 356)　　　　JANUARY 17

Born at Coman in Upper Egypt of well-to-do parents, Anthony was about twenty years old when he heard the scripture passage, "If you wish to be perfect, go and sell all that you have and give it to the poor." Anthony took the instruction seriously and literally, giving away the considerable fortune he had just inherited after the death of his mother and father. He became a hermit, finding God in a tomb near his native village. He lived there for twenty years, never seeing another person. His food was thrown to him over a wall.

Later he established the first religious community such as we know today, by gathering together a large group of hermits into a loosely knit colony.

Apparently during his lifetime there was an epidemic of erysipelas, an intense inflammation of the skin accompanied by fever, for it was called St. Anthony's fire, and his name is still invoked against skin diseases.

Anthony became famous throughout all Egypt and beyond, being called upon to advise people of every rank. He lived a life full of temptations and conflicts with demons in the shape of wild beasts, disciplining himself all the while with self-denial, fasting, prayer, and good works. He died at the age of one hundred and five, his grave site kept secret by those who buried him in accordance with Anthony's request.

ST. ANTHONY of Padua (1195 - 1231)   JUNE 13

Born of noble, powerful, God-fearing parents, Anthony was gifted with a quick understanding and prodigious memory. As a youth he was studious and virtuous, but also a young man of flesh and blood, and it was in an effort to overcome the temptations of his body that he sought the help of his faith.

Shortly after entering the priesthood, he was stricken down with a severe illness and was unable to pursue his desire to be a missionary. Instead he developed his most unusual gift for speaking to become an eloquent orator. He had a loud and clear voice, a winning smile, a pleasing countenance, and profound learning. His message was strong and fearless, merciless toward oppressors of the weak and defenseless. Acknowledged to be one of the greatest preachers, he supplemented his sermons with magical illustrations—a school of fish crowded the river bank to listen to him as a lesson to the inattentive heretics, a hobgoblin induced a young friar to return a borrowed book, and a disrespectful listener's mule knelt before the sacrament as a lesson to his master.

As a miracle worker he earned unlimited popularity, and some believers in his marvelous powers have a prayer which begins, "O God, pray to St. Anthony for us."

He died at the age of thirty six, worn out from preaching the message of God's infinite love.

and search thoroughly as I look for what I have lost or misplaced. If I cannot recover the missing article, help me to understand that it is not as important as a loss of faith, a loss of love, or the loss of confidence in my ability to get better organized and to be more careful so that I can prevent more such incidents in the future.

PRAYER OF PETITION

O wondrous Saint Anthony, glorious by reason of the fame of thy miracles, obtain for me this favor that I desire from the bottom of my heart. Thou who wast so gracious unto poor sinners, regard not the lack of merit on the part of the one who calls upon thee, but consider the glory of God, which will be exalted once more through thee, to the salvation of my soul and the granting of the petition that I now make with such ardent yearning. ——————— (state request) As a pledge of my gratitude, I beg thee to accept my promise to live henceforth more agreeably to the teachings of God, and to be devoted to the service of the poor. Bless this resolution and obtain for me the grace to be faithful thereto even until death.

PRAYER OF THANKSGIVING

O glorious wonder-worker, Saint Anthony, father of the poor and comforter of the afflicted, thou hast come with such loving solicitude to my assistance, and hast comforted me so abundantly: behold me at thy feet to offer thee my heartfelt thanks. Accept my promise which I now renew, to live always in the love of Jesus and my neighbor. Continue to shield me with thy protection, and obtain for me the grace of being able one day to enter the kingdom of heaven, there to sing with thee the everlasting mercies of God.

† † † † † † † † †

ST. APOLLONIA (3rd century)   FEBRUARY 9

Nothing reliable is known of Apollonia's early life, but one legend is that, when she was only a small child, an angel took her from her family and presented her to one of St. Anthony's disciples, who promptly baptized her, dressed her in white, and took her to Alexandria to preach. Her father went to the police about the abduction and, presumably, she was returned home for some period of time.

Many years later, as an aged deaconess, she was attacked by an Alexandrian mob during a riot against the Christians. She was seized and beaten by a soldier who, angered by her refusal to play homage to a pagan image, tore out her teeth one by one. The blood ran down his arms, but Apollonia uttered not a single cry. Shortly thereafter, she was led to the stake and burned.

† † † † † † † † †

ST. AUGUSTINE (354 - 430)   AUGUST 28

His father was a pagan landowner, Fatricius, and his mother was a devout Christian, St. Monica. Born into a pagan world which was gradually turning Christian, the conflict of his youth was between the tangible pleasures of paganism and the intangible joys of Christianity.

A gifted, precocious child, he became a brilliant scholar. At the University of Carthage, Augustine was the gayest, most sensual and most egotistic student. He was dedicated to self-gratification, self-advancement, and self-expression. His personal life was wild and full of transgressions. He had a son by his mistress with whom he lived for ten or twelve years. But he became entangled in many difficulties—financial worries, thwarted ambitions, frustrations in friendships, and misunderstandings in love. He began to examine himself and, from his own Confessions we know the scripture which led him to serenity, "Not in rioting and drunkenness, not in chambering and wantonness, not in strife and envying, but put ye on the Lord Jesus Christ."

At the age of twenty eight, Augustine met St. Ambrose and was later baptized by him. Augustine was a respected teacher of rhetoric and public speaking, a natural leader, and writer of over one hundred works which deal with philosophy, history, morals, and spirituality .

One of Augustine's remarks reveal dramatically his struggle between his life of pleasure and one of service to God and others. His cry from the heart was, "God, make me chaste, but not yet."

ST. AUGUSTINE'S PRAYER FOR STRENGTH
Give me whatever you ask of me,
then ask of me what you will, Lord.
Remember that we are only dust,
for of the dust you made us.
But I can do anything in Him who strengthens me;
Lord, strengthen me, and I can do everything.
Give me whatever you ask of me,
then ask of me what you will.

† † † † † † † † †

ST. BALBINA (1st century)   MARCH 31

Allegedly the daughter of Blessed Quirinus, Balbina was perhaps baptized by Pope Alexander, and is buried on the Appian Way near her father.

Though the reason is unknown, Balbina is invoked for the cure or prevention of lymph gland diseases.

† † † † † † † † † †

ST. BALTHASAR (1st century)   JANUARY 11

Reputedly one of the three Magi, "the wise men from the East," who came to adore the baby Jesus in Bethlehem. Some say they were kings, some magicians, and even their names vary in different sources. Generally the three are given as Sts. Gaspar, Melchior, and Balthasar.

† † † † † † † † † †

ST. BARBARA (3rd century)   DECEMBER 4

The legends say that Barbara was either Syrian or Egyptian, daughter of a rich heathen by the name of Dioscorus. A young maiden of great beauty, Barbara had many suitors and her father had her banished to a tower to discourage the attentions of the young men who wished to win her hand in marriage.

In the tower, Barbara had three windows installed to represent the Holy Trinity, rather than the two which her father had instructed the workmen to build. Because of this, Dioscorus found out she was Christian and attempted to kill her, but she was miraculously transported out through the window and disappeared into a rock. The authorities were notified and she was eventually captured and tortured, after which her father came to put her to death himself. He beheaded her, but on his way home he was struck by lightning and reduced to ashes.

PRAYER FOR PROTECTION

O holy Christian protector, Saint Barbara, open your heart for those who are weak. Strengthen me with thy faith and protect me with thy mighty strength. Save me from all harm, I pray.

† † † † † † † † † †

ST. BARNABAS (1st century)   JUNE 11

Born in Cyprus, a Jew of the tribe of Levi, and named Joseph, he probably spent much time in Jerusalem, possibly owning property there. He converted to Christianity and was given the name Barnabas which means "son of consolation" because of his kind and optimistic nature. He sold his estate and gave the money to the apostles. Later he accompanied St. Paul to the cities of Asia Minor where, on at least one occasion, Paul was thought to be the Greek god Mercury, and Barnabas to be Jupiter.

St. Luke says that Barnabas "was a good man, full of the Holy Ghost and of Faith." His tenderness and kind heart were among the most noticable characteristics of his personal life.

✝ ✝ ✝ ✝ ✝ ✝ ✝ ✝ ✝

ST. BARTHALOMEW (1st century)   AUGUST 24

His name is found in the lists of the apostles, but nowhere else in the New Testament. It is possible that he is the person mentioned as Nathanael, and who the Lord praised for his innocence and simplicity of heart. Legend says that he later preached in Egypt, Persia, Mesopotamia, and was martyred in India by being skinned alive.

✝ ✝ ✝ ✝ ✝ ✝ ✝ ✝ ✝

ST. BASIL (330 - 379)   JUNE 14

Basil was one of ten children, born into the church's most remarkable family of saints. His paternal grandparents, his mother, father, two of his brothers, and one sister are all honored as saints.

Though small and weak in body, he was a sturdy and vigorous bishop, a persuasive preacher, a dedicated defender of the faith, and a prolific writer of books, letters, treatises, poems, and commentaries.

PRAYER FOR JUSTICE

O Glorious Saint Basil, grant me thy strength and protection. Make that which is evil good, and preserve the just in their righteousness. For thou can do all things and will surely save those who are worthy from oppression and injustice. For those who desire liberation, thou will set free. Bless me this day, I pray.

ST. BASIL'S PRAYER FOR PURIFICATION

Lord our God, great, eternal, wonderful in glory,
who keepest covenant and promises for those
that love Thee with their whole heart,
who art the life of all,
the help of those that flee unto Thee,
cleanse us from our sins, secret and open;
and from every thought displeasing to Thy goodness,
cleanse our bodies and souls,
our hearts and consciences,
that with a pure heart, and a clear soul,
with perfect love and calm hope,
we may venture confidently and fearlessly to pray unto thee.

† † † † † † † † †

ST. BEDE (673 - 735)   MAY 25

Bede entered the abbey as a child and spent his life, as one associate described him, "always writing, praying, reading, teaching." A simple, pious man, Bede became the first great English historian. He wrote forty books, including a good deal of verse. Becoming blind in his later years did not deter him from his work and, on the day of his death, he was still busy dictating a translation of the Gospel of St. John to a secretary. In the evening the boy who was writing said to Bede, "There is still one sentence which is not written down." And when it was done, the boy told him it was finished. "Thou hast spoken truth, it is finished," replied Bede, and died quietly.

ST. BEDE'S PRAYER FOR A HOLY LIFE

Open our hearts, O Lord,
and enlighten us by the grace of your Holy Spirit,
that we may always seek what is pleasing to you
and order our lives after your commandments
that we may be worthy to enter into your unending joy.

ST. BEDE'S PRAYER FOR RICH AND POOR

O God that art the sole hope of the world,
The only refuge for unhappy men,
Abiding in the faithfulness of Heaven,
Give me a strong succur in this testing-place,
O King, protect Thy man from utter ruin,
Lest the weak flesh surrender to the tyrant,
Facing innumerable blows alone.
Remember I am dust and wind and shadow,
And life is fleeting as the flower of the grass.

But may the eternal mercy which hath shone from time of old
Rescue Thy servant from the jaws of the lie.
Thou who didst come from on high in the cloak of the flesh,
Strike down the dragon with the two-edged sword
Whereby our mortal flesh can war with the winds
And break down strongholds, with our Captain, God.

† † † † † † † † †

ST. BENEDICT (480 - 550)   MARCH 21

Born in central Italy, he was sent to school when he was about fourteen. Shocked at the corrupt customs of his schoolmates, he fled to Rome and joined a community of religious students. After a while he left them and made his way into the desert wilderness where he lived alone in a cave for three years.

About 530 he founded an abbey on the road to Naples and lived there until his death. All we know of his personality shows him to be a strong, but pleasant and friendly man. He became famous as a wonder-worker before he died standing at the altar with outstretched arms.

ST. BENEDICT'S PRAYER FOR SEEKERS OF FAITH
Gracious and holy Father,
give us the wisdom to discover you,
the intelligence to understand you,
the diligence to seek after you,
the patience to wait for you,
eyes to behold you,
a heart to meditate on you,
and a life to proclaim you,
through the power of the spirit of Jesus, our Lord.

† † † † † † † † †

ST. BERNADETTE (1844 - 1879)   APRIL 16

Bernadette Soubirous was born at Lourdes, the oldest daughter of a poor miller. She was always a frail, sensitive girl, simple and uneducated. She was fourteen years old when, between February 11 and July 16, 1858, she had a series of remarkable experiences. On eighteen occasions Bernadette saw a young and beautiful lady appear in the hollow of a rock on the bank of the river. While others were present at the time of the appearances, only Bernadette seemed to see and hear the lady who eventually identified herself as the Virgin

Mary under the title of "the Immaculate Conception."

In 1866 Bernadette entered the convent of the Sisters of Charity at Nevers where she lived with humble simplicity until her death at the age of thirty five.

Since the apparitions at Lourdes, many millions of pilgrims have visited the Grotto and thousands of miracles are believed to have taken place there. Now over two million visitors come there each year.

PRAYER FOR HEALING

Blessed Mother, and Glorious Saint Bernadette, through thy intercession, bless those who are sick, infirm, injured, or suffering. Ease their pain and torment, heal the wounds, mend the hurt. Let them see the light of love, the joy of understanding, and the peace of serenity in the knowledge of thy care.

† † † † † † † † †

ST. BERNARD of Montjour (996 - 1081)   MAY 28

A descendant of a rich and noble family, Bernard received a thorough education before entering the service of the church. For forty two years he served the people of the Alps, clearing the trails of highway robbers and building rest homes for travellers at the top of the two Alpine passes now known as Great and Little St. Bernard. It is also after St. Bernard that those great compassionate dogs which were sent out to rescue stranded mountain travellers are named.

ST. BERNARD'S PRAYER FOR GOD'S LOVE

O God,
your greatness knows no bounds,
your peace goes beyond all understanding,
your love surpasses all reckoning.
Help us to love you
if not as you have first loved us,
then to the fullness of our power to love.
And strengthen and deepen this power
so that we may love you more and more.

PRAYER FOR SPECIAL FAVORS

I bring this request to you, Blessed Saint Bernard, for your assistance. Add your mighty strength to my own efforts to cause this prayer to be answered. The favor I ask will bring harm to no one, and only benefits can come from its fulfillment.

† † † † † † † † †

ST. BLAISE (3rd century)   FEBRUARY 3

Legends abound about this great healer and miracle worker Born in Armenia, he became Bishop of Sebastea. He was by profession a doctor, and the sick came to him, animals as well as people. He cured them all and sent them away. It is said that, when the animals came to be cured, they would wait patiently and not disturb him if he were at his prayers, no matter how dire their own need for healing.

During the persecution under Licinius, Blaise was taken prisoner. It was while he was in jail that he miraculously cured a child who had a fish bone caught in his throat. Blaise was left in prison to starve to death but a woman killed her pig which previously Blaise had saved from a wolf, and brought him the meat to eat. It was after this that his guards killed him, it is said, by pulling the flesh off his body with an iron comb.

Having great powers over throat ailments, the faithful believe Blaise can cure such conditions quickly. Kneel and touch the throat gently with the unlighted end of a burning candle and pray, "May the Lord deliver you from the evils of the throat, and from every other evil."

To remove thorns or splinters embedded in the flesh, rub the area gently with the fingers and pray, "Saint Blaise commands thee come forth." Repeat several times if necessary.

> PRAYER FOR REMOVING OBSTRUCTIONS IN THE THROAT
> Place both hands loosely around the neck and pray, "Blessed Blaise, martyr and servant of Jesus Christ, commands thee to pass up or down, by the law of the all powerful, go down or come out."
> † † † † † † † † †

ST. CAMILLUS de Lellis (1550 - 1614)   JULY 18

A huge 6'6" soldier, Camillus went off at the age of seventeen with the Venetian army to fight the Turks, but abscesses in both his feet disabled him. He was admitted to a hospital in Rome as a patient and servant, but his violent temper and his passion for card playing got him into trouble.

Gambling was Camillus's sin, bringing shame and destitution. He reached the point where he had lost every penny he had, plus his

22

gun, and even his shirt. In order to survive he took a job building a new monastery, and there the example of the monks had a beneficial effect on him. He was converted, and went back to the same hospital where he had been a patient, thereafter serving the sick and dying for about forty years.

He tended the patients at the Incurables Hospital in Rome, and founded the Servants of the Sick, a congregation of priests whose purpose was to serve all the sick, even those striken with plague. Camillus' feet and legs bothered him all his life, and when the time came that he could no longer walk, he would drag himself from bed to bed to see to the patients' needs.

Favors are granted to those faithful who honor Saint Camillus with prayers for seven successive Sundays.

† † † † † † † † †

ST. CATHERINE of Alexandria (3rd century)   NOVEMBER 25
While the facts are doubtful, the legends about this beautiful and talented princess are marvelous. A pagan by birth, she became interested in Christianity through her studies and converted to it after seeing Our Lady and the Baby Jesus in a vision.

According to accounts, by the time Catherine was seventeen she had learned everything there was to know from the schools and libraries of Alexandria. In an effort to discredit her, Emperor Maximinus, who was violently persecuting Christians, called forth fifty scholars to debate her, but she emerged victorious. Then he tried to seduce her, but she rejected him and was flung into prison. She was condemned to death by being broken on a spiked wheel, but when she was bound to it, the wheel broke and flew into many pieces which struck and killed her executioner and numerous spectators who had come to watch her die. She was finally beheaded with the sword at the age of eighteen.

PRAYER TO GET A HUSBAND
Sweet St. Catherine, send me a husband,
A good one, I pray,
But any one better than none.
Oh, St. Catherine, lend me thine aid,
That I may not die an old maid.

† † † † † † † † †

ST. CATHERINE of Bologna (1412 - 1463)   MARCH 9

When she was ten years old, her father sent her to court as a companion to the Princess Margarita. Here she pursued the study of literature and the fine arts. After the princess married, Catherine turned her back on court life and joined a community of devout maidens in a neighboring town.

Though temptations often tried her patience, her humility, and her faith, she remained faithful to her three rules of life—speak well of everyone, practice constant humility, and do not meddle in the affairs of others.

† † † † † † † † †

ST. CATHERINE of Sweden (1331 - 1381)   MARCH 24

The fourth daughter of Ulf, prince of Nericia, and St. Bridget, Catherine married Count Edgard when she was about fourteen years old. It was a happy union and both Catherine and Edgard devoted themselves to church service. After about four years, Catherine went to visit her mother in Rome, and just a short time after then her husband died suddenly. So Catherine remained with her mother for twenty years, a willing helper in St. Bridget's pilgrimages, devotions, and works of charity.

Never known to speak an unkind or impatient word, Catherine shunned gossip, saying that "both the tale bearer and the one who listens carry the devil on their tongues."

† † † † † † † † †

ST. CECILIA (3rd century)   NOVEMBER 22

A cultured young aristocrat, and a Christian from infancy, Cecilia's parents gave her in marriage to a noble pagan youth, Valerianus. She immediately converted him and he was baptized by the pope. Valerianus in turn converted his brother, Tiburtius, and together they distributed goods to the poor and buried the bodies of those who were killed by the official, Turius Almachius, who was persecuting the Christians. The two brothers were arrested and executed. Because Cecilia buried them, she was also arrested. The judge condemned her to be suffocated in the bath of her own house. But when she remained unhurt in the overheated room, he had her decapitated. The executioner let his sword fall three times, without separating her head from her body. He fled, leaving Cecilia bathed in her own blood. After three days she died.

Buried in Rome, her crypt was opened nearly 1,800 years after burial, and her body was fresh and sweet-smelling. Cecilia lay there as if peacefully at sleep.

† † † † † † † † †

ST. CHRISTOPHER (3rd century)   JULY 25

In Greek legend, he was a barbarous cannibal. In Latin legend, he was a giant about eighteen feet tall who carried a tree as a walking stick when he strolled the fields and roads. His origins are unknown and, beyond the belief that he may have been beheaded in Asia Minor under the persecution reign of Emperor Decius, nothing of his true life has been recorded.

However, the legends are many and colorful. One is that he found God only after serving the most powerful king on earth. While singing a song to the king, Christopher noticed that the king crossed himself every time the devil was mentioned in the lyrics. Christopher asked him why, and the king said he was afraid of the devil. So Christopher left the king's service to find the devil so he could work for the most powerful one. He did find the devil and enlisted in his service, only to notice that whenever they passed a cross, the devil trembled. Christopher questioned him, and the devil admitted that he was afraid of Christ. So Christopher left the devil to search for a more powerful master and, after finding a holy hermit who instructed him in service to God, joined the Lord's forces.

When told that he must fast, he said he was afraid he would lose his strength, and when told he must pray, he was too proud. So he was given the task of carrying people, for God's sake, across a raging stream. One day he was carrying a child who grew so heavy that it seemed to him as if he had the whole world on his shoulders. It was later revealed to him that it was the Christ Child he transported, and the weighty burden was the world's troubles which Jesus bore.

An ancient rhyme tells of Christopher's protection:
If thou the face of Christopher on any morn shall see,
Through the day from sudden death thou shalt preserved be.

ST. CLARE of Assisi (1193 - 1253)   AUGUST 12

The eldest daughter of the Count of Sasso-Rosso, Clare was a child endowed with rare virtues and most devoted to prayer. At the age of eighteen, she heard St. Francis preach and left home to live the religious life. Francis provided her refuge, cut off her hair, and gave her a garment of rough brown wool to wear.

Clare founded the Order of Poor Ladies, or Poor Clares as it was called, where the nuns went barefoot, spoke only when necessary, and had no property. Clare was a "saint among saints" being humble, merciful, charming, courteous, and optimistic. She spent much of the night in prayer and, after her devotions, engaged in manual labor.

When St. Francis died, and his body was being carried into the chapel, Clare washed it with her tears and covered the sacred stigmata with kisses. Twenty six years later, when she lay near death, she was heard to murmur, "depart in peace, for the road thou has followed is the good one." An attending sister asked to whom she was speaking and she replied, "I am speaking to my departing soul and he who was its guide is not far away." There is little doubt that it was St. Francis who had come to lead her to heaven.

ST. CLEMENT of Rome (1st century)   NOVEMBER 23

The third successor of St. Peter, Clement governed as Pope Clement I for about ten years before his death about 97 AD. His origins are unclear. Various sources believe he may have been a Jew, or a freed slave, or the son of a freed slave. It is known that he was well educated for at least one of his writings, Letter to the Corinthians, has been authenticated. It ends with this powerful prayer for all mankind.

"God of all flesh, who givest life and death,
thou who castest down the insolence of the proud and turnest
aside the scheming of men, be our help!
Oh, Master, appease the hunger of the indigent;
Deliver the fallen among us.
God, good and merciful, forget our sins,
our wrongdoing and backsliding;
take no account of the faults of thy servants.
Give us concord and peace, as to all the inhabitants of the earth.
It is from thee that our princes and those who govern us
here below hold their power;
grant them health, peace, concord, stability;
direct their counsels in the way of goodness.
Thou alone canst do all this and confer on us still greater benefits.
We proclaim it by the high priest and master of our soul, Jesus Christ,
by whom to thee be all glory and power, now and in endless ages."

† † † † † † † † †

ST. COLUMBA (521 - 597)   JUNE 9

Born an Irishman of royal blood, he may have become a King of Ireland, but instead he became the most famous of the saints of Scotland. After an intemperate youth and an inclination toward violence, he softened and became a travelling priest.

The people were greatly impressed by his miracles, including the driving away of a water monster from the River Ness by making the sign of the cross. He was also credited with the power to foretell future events.

He was an indefatigable worker, every hour being passed with prayer, writing, or work. One writer said he "had the face of an angel. He was of an excellent nature, polished in speech, holy in deed, great in counsel, and loving unto all."

† † † † † † † † †

ST. CONCORDIA (3rd century)   AUGUST 13

Although there is doubt about the accuracy of the accounts, it is thought that Concordia was the childhood nurse of the soldier, Hippolytus, who guarded St. Lawrence when he was imprisoned. Lawrence converted Hippolytus who, in turn, converted Concordia.

† † † † † † † † †

STS. COSMAS and DAMIAN (3rd century)　　　SEPTEMBER 27

Cosmas and his twin brother, Damian, were born in Arabia. They were physicians by profession and came to Syria to practice the art of healing, treating the sickness of the soul and delivering the possessed, as well as curing the illness of the body. They took no payment for their services and soon became known as "the silverless" or "the moneyless ones." They brought many to the Christian faith, and when the Diocletian persecution began, they were arrested. Miraculously they suffered no injury from water, fire, air, nor on the cross, and were finally beheaded with the sword.

† † † † † † † † †

STS. CRISPIN and CRISPINIAN (3rd century)　　　OCTOBER 25

Although they were noble Romans, the two brothers worked as shoemakers in disguise so that they could carry the message of their faith without attracting undue attention. Since they worked free, their clientele became considerable.

However, during the Diocletian persecution, the brothers were arrested and, after refusing to turn from their faith, they were subjected to the most heinous cruelty. They were stretched on the rack, thongs were cut from their flesh, and nails were driven through their fingers. A millstone was then fastened about the neck of each, and they were thrown into the river, but they swam ashore. They were immersed in boiling water, plunged into molten lead, and an attempt to burn them at the stake was made. Death came only when they were beheaded.

† † † † † † † † †

ST. CUTHBERT (7th century)　　　MARCH 20

As a youth, Cuthbert tended his father's sheep. When he was about fifteen, he had a vision of angels conducting a soul to heaven. After this, he embraced the religious life, serving twelve years as prior of an abbey, then living as a hermit for eight years on a small island.

He was a man of extraordinary charm and practical ability, attracting the people by the beauty of his holiness. His fame as a miracle worker grew, including one occasion when he is believed to have healed a dying baby with a kiss. There is also a legend that Cuthbert stood in the icy sea waters to recite the whole Book of Psalms. When he finished, he came ashore and two seals followed him, placing themselves across his feet so that he would be warmed quickly.

† † † † † † † † †

ST. CYRIACUS (4th century)   AUGUST 8

Cyriacus is credited with delivering Artemis, Diacletian's daughter, from possession by a demon. After this event, both Artemis and her mother were converted to Christianity, but Diacletian continued his persecution of the Christians.

Later the King of Persia's daughter fell under the power of evil forces and Cyriacus is said to have cured and converted her.

Diocletain found Cyriacus carrying food and water to Christians who were being made to build baths for the Roman emperor and condemned him to a particularly barbeous death. The rope, the wooden horse, the bath of pit, and interminable flogging were all used before he died.

PRAYER TO DELIVER THE POSSESSED

Blessed Saint Cyriacus, your powers to redeem souls and liberate the spirit from satanic forces through your prayers, penances, and blessings are well-known. I humbly ask for your intercession before our Lord, Jesus Christ, because I want to be worthy of the Holy Spirit that can lead from darkness to the light of the eternal kingdom, forever and ever.

† † † † † † † † †

ST. DIONYSIUS (1st century)   OCTOBER 9

This is Denis the Areopagite who was converted at Athens by St. Paul, as referred to in Acts 17:34, after hearing Paul speak of the resurrection of the dead. He became first bishop of Athens, and died a martyr under Decius about 95 AD.

This saint was later confused with St. Denis of Paris, who was beheaded under the persecution of Valerian in 258. And, through another series of confusions, identified with a philosopher-theologian, now called Pseudo-Dionysius, who was a 5th century Greek writer.

ST. DIONYSIUS' LOVE PRAYER

O God the Father, good beyond all that is good, fair beyond all that is fair, in whom is calmness, peace, and concord; do thou make up the dissensions which divide us from each other, and bring us back into a unity of love which may bear some likeness to thy divine nature. And as thou art above all things, make us one by the unanimity of a good mind; that through the embrace of charity and the bonds of affection, we may be spiritually one, as well in ourselves as in each other; through that peace of thine which maketh all things peaceful, and through the grace, mercy, and tenderness of thy Son, Jesus Christ.

† † † † † † † † †

ST. DYMPNA (6th century)   MAY 15

Legends say Dympna was the beautiful daughter of a pagan king of Ireland. After the death of her mother, her father wanted to marry his own daughter, but Dympna fled to Belgium. She was pursued, captured, and beheaded by her father.

For reasons not clear, she has always been invoked as patroness against insanity, and has been credited with numerous miraculous cures.

PRAYER ON BEHALF OF THOSE WITH
NERVOUS CONDITIONS

Lord Jesus, grant that, through the prayers of this youthful martyr of purity, Dympna, those who suffer from nervous and mental illness everywhere on earth may be helped and consoled. I recommend to you in particular ————— (mention by name those you are praying for). Give them patience to bear with their affliction and resignation to your divine will. Give them the consolation they need and, if it be your will, the cure they so much desire.

† † † † † † † † †

ST. ELIGIUS (588 - 660)   DECEMBER 1

A native of Limoges, Eligius' father recognized his talent early and sent him to work with Abbo, master of the mint. His genius for engraving was developed and eventually he was appointed master of the mint at Paris under King Clotaire II. Elgious was ambitious and under Dagobert I, the son of Cloitaire II, he became one of the king's most influential counsellors. Though he was powerful and sought after, he spent much of his time coming to the aid of anyone in need, ransoming captives, freeing prisoners, and distributing clothes to the poor.

Numerous works of art were attributed to him, including the tomb of St. Denis which he decorated with his gold work.

† † † † † † † † †

ST. ERASMUS (3rd century)   JUNE 2
The only facts known are that he was a bishop of Formiae in Campania and was martyred under Diocletian's persecutions.

The legend of his death, however, makes his life more colorful. He was killed by having his stomach torn open and his intestines wound out of his body on a windlass. Since a windlass is a horizontal bar which is turned by a crank, similar to the device that is used to raise a ship's anchor, Erasmas was taken as patron of sailors, and protector against various stomach diseases.

† † † † † † † † †

ST. EUSTACE (2nd century)   SEPTEMBER 20
While nothing certain is known about him, there is a marvelous legend of Eustace and his wife, Theopista. Eustace commanded the emperor's armies and had an immense fortune. The couple served pagan gods, and brought up their two sons in luxury and virture.

One day Eustace was deer hunting, and was converted by the vision of a stag with a crucifix between its antlers. At the same time, at their home an apparition appeared to Theopista and revealed to her the virtue of Christianity. The next day the entire family was baptized.

But soon misfortune overtook Eustace. All of his servants died of plague. Epidemic killed all his cattle. Soldiers robbed his home, and the family had to flee. They took a boat to Egypt, but since Eustace has no money to pay the fare, on their arrival the captain kept Theopista as hostage. Her abuse was only prevented by the captain's sudden death. The two children were carried off, one by a lion and one by a wolf, but shepherds came in time to rescue and adopt them.

After fifteen years the barbarians invaded, and the emperor searched and found Eustace working on a farm. He made him commander-in-chief of his armies again, and the enemy was defeated. All the family, including the two sons who were now soldiers, were reunited in time to take part in the victory celebrations. However, these festivities were to be followed by sacrifices to the idols, and since the family would not participate in the pagan rites, they were all delivered to the lions to be eaten. The lions would not attack so they were all put into a bronze bull, roasted over a slow fire for three days, and perished together without their bodies being consumed.

† † † † † † † † †

ST. EXPEDITUS (4th century)   APRIL 19
There is no evidence that there ever was such a saint. The name could have come from the word "expedite" which is used when matters should be taken care of promptly. Some say it originated when a box of various saints' relics were sent from Rome to Paris. The box bore the word "expedito," which means "to send off." The word was mistaken for the name of a particular saint.

PRAYER IN ANY EMERGENCY
I call upon thee, St. Expeditus, in my day of trouble with confidence that you will be my help and my strength. Bring to me justice if my cause is just, triumph in my battle if my struggle is right, and hasty assistance as my need is urgent. Be my light in the darkness and my guide toward the pathway which will turn my enemies away from me so that I may live in peace, in love, and in praise of God.

† † † † † † † † †

STS. FAITH, HOPE and CHARITY (1st century)   OCTOBER 6
There is no evidence that these sisters are anything but legendary. However, these virtues are sure to be needed by all from time to time.

There are similar myths in Greek and in Latin of three young girls, ages twelve, ten, and nine, respectively.

In Greek the sisters are Pistis, Elpis and Agape, daughters of Sophia.

In Latin the sisters are Fides, Spes, and Caritas, daughters of Sapientia.

In English they are Faith, Hope, and Charity, daughters of St. Wisdom, and they, along with their mother, were martyred in Rome under Hadrian about 120.

PRAYER FOR FAITH, HOPE, and CHARITY

Glorious Saint Faith, I ask that I ever find you at my side, giving me faith in my hours of need, even unto the moment of my death. Saint Hope, remain beside me always, instilling thy confidence, hope, and trust in my heart. Saint Charity, wherever I go, let me show kindness and generosity toward the poor, the lonely, the desperate, and all in need.

† † † † † † † † †

ST. FELICITAS of Rome (2nd century)   JULY 10

While it is not necessarily a true story, the legend of a pious Roman widow with seven sons is both colorful and inspiring.

Felicitas' seven sons (called the Seven Brothers and they are commemorated as martyrs on this same feast day) were Januarius, Felix, Philip, Sylvanus, Alexander, Vitalis, and Martial.

Felicitas was a socially prominent woman and because she was in the public eye, the pagan priest ordered her to pay homage to the heathen gods. She refused and was put on trial along with her sons. Convicted, they were all condemned to die. Januarius was whipped to death with a leaded whip. Felix and Philip were beaten to death with staves. Silvanus was thrown over a precipice. Alexander, Martial, and Vitalis, along with Felicitas, were beheaded.

† † † † † † † † †

ST. FELIX of Nola (3rd century)   JANUARY 14

Son of a Romano-Syrian soldier, Felix settled near Naples where he owned some property. He became a priest and served the bishop, St. Maximus, during the persecution under Decius. After the bishop was executed, Felix continued his life of service to the poor.

At one time, when he was being pursued in a search for Christians, he "crept through a hole in a ruinous wall which was instantly closed up by spider's webs" and escaped being caught.

† † † † † † † † †

ST. FIACRE (7th century)   AUGUST 30

An Irish priest who longed for solitude, Fiacre came to France and was given land by St. Faro. On the land he built a hospice to receive travellers and a cell in which he himself lived. He remained there the rest of his life, dividing his time between prayer, the work of his hands, and care of the poor.

Because of an incident with a meddlesome woman who spoke against him to St. Faro, Fiacre excluded all women from his enclosure, and there are many stories of misfortune which befell those who trespassed, even after his death.

His fame for miracles was widespread. All manner of diseases were cured by laying on his hands—blindness, fevers, and especially tumors.

† † † † † † † † †

ST. FRANCES of Rome (1384 - 1440)   MARCH 9

Born in Rome of a wealthy family, she married Lorenzo de Ponziani when she was only twelve years old, and lived with him for forty years as a model of fidelity and devotion to her home and children. She was remarkable for her humility and detachment during her many trials, including the deaths of her children, her husband's banishment, and the loss of all her property.

She was never known to quarrel with her husband, and believed that a married woman must not forget she is a homemaker, and sometimes "she must leave God at the altar to find him in her housework."

One of the greatest mystics of the fifteenth century, Frances was a much loved, wonder-working saint. She practiced her faith, cared for the sick, gave alms to the needy, and was favored by God with visible presence of her guardian angel who comforted her in times of sorrow, guided her in times of danger, and even chastised her when she deserved it. Her powers included reading consciences, detecting diabolical plots, and foretelling the future—including her death on a day she had foretold.

† † † † † † † † †

ST. FRANCIS BORGIA (1510 - 1572)   OCTOBER 10

Born near Valencia, Spain, Francis was not happy with his ancestry for he was from the infamous Borgia family. His grandfather, Juan Borgia, the second son of Alexander VI, was assassinated in Rome on June 14, 1497, by an unknown hand, and his family always believed the killer to be Caesar Borgia.

Francis was reared at the court of Charles V. At the age of nineteen he married Eleanor de Castro. They had eight children and, until his wife's death in 1546, Francis devoted himself to duties at the emperor's court and on his own estate.

After Eleanor's death, he withdrew from court, settled all his worldly and family affairs, and entered the Society of Jesus. He was ordained three months later, and became known as The Holy Duke, but he practiced the utmost humility. He preached successfully, and helped protect St. Theresa of Avila from her persecutors when her confessor insisted that her visitations were wiles of the devil. Francis was the typical saint of the Spanish nobility—courteous, refined, kind, humble, and generous, yet most determined and enterprising. He died in 1572, two days after his return to Rome from an unsuccessful mission to the Kings of Spain and France to enlist their support for a crusade against the Turks.

† † † † † † † † †

ST. FRANCIS DE SALES (1567 - 1622)   JANUARY 29

The firstborn of cultured and influential parents, Francis was the eldest of thirteen children. With his father's encouragement he studied law, but chose the priesthood and dedication to the poor rather than a legal career.

He set out to preach among the Calvinists and made over eight thousand converts within two years. He was known for his meekness and humility. His motto was "to ask for nothing and to refuse nothing." He wrote profusely. There are at least four hundred editions of his masterpiece, Introduction to the Devout Life. His Treatise on the Love of God took ten years to write, and there are thousands of letters extant.

Francis approved of dancing, regarding the beauties of art as a mystic ladder toward God. His basic premise was that "God is the God of the human heart."

† † † † † † † † †

ST. FRANCIS of Assisi (1181 - 1226)   OCTOBER 4

Son of a wealthy cloth merchant, Francis led a carefree, pleasure seeking life in his youth, taking part in street battles and military adventures, and spending long months in the jails of Perugia. He had a ready wit, sang merrily, loved pleasure, and delighted in fine clothes.

In his early twenties, Francis was praying in church one day when he heard an image of Christ speak to him. "Go, Francis, and repair my house, which as you see is falling into ruin." Taking the words literally, Francis sold some of his father's goods and used the money to repair the church. Because of this, his father disinherited and disowned him.

But Francis had found his vocation and dedicated himself to serving through his truly promiscious love. Francis felt every creature was a word from God . . . he talked to birds, reasoned with the wolf, tended the lepers, healed the sick. He was enthusiastic about everything except sin. A man of tremendous spiritual insight and a chivalrous character, he was blessed with poetic gifts, charm, simplicity, compassion, good manners, and an honesty and all-embracing love that made him in the words of Benedict XI, ". . . the most perfect image of Christ that ever was."

On September 24, 1224, while he was praying, scars appeared on his body, corresponding to the five wounds of the crucified Jesus. This is the gift of the stigmata and is taken as a message direct from Christ. The wounds never left him, and were one of the sources of the weakness and pain he suffered increasingly until his death on October 4, 1226.

Today, it is said that a white flower grows beside the Basilica of

St. Francis at Assisi and blooms, unreasonably, all year round.

ST. FRANCIS' PRAYER

Lord, make me an instrument of your peace.
Where there is hatred, let me sow love.
Where there is injury, pardon.
Where there is doubt, faith.
Where there is despair, hope.
Where there is darkness, light.
And where there is sadness, joy.
O Divine Master, grant that I may not so much seek to be consoled,
      as to console,
To be understood, as to understand,
To be loved, as to love,
For it is in giving that we receive,
It is in pardoning that we are pardoned,
And it is in dying that we are born to eternal life.

ST. FRANCIS' PRAYER TO THE SACRED HEART

May Your Heart dwell always in our hearts!
May Your Blood ever flow in the veins of our souls!
O sun of our hearts,
You give life to all things by the rays of Your goodness!
I will not go until Your Heart has strengthened me,
O Lord Jesus!
May the Heart of Jesus be the King of my heart!
Blessed by God.

ST. FRANCIS' CANTICLE OF THE SUN

Oh Most High, Almighty, Good Lord God,
to Thee belong praise, glory, honor and all blessing.
Praised be my Lord God, with all His creatures,
and especially our brother the Sun,
who brings us the day and who brings us the light:
fair is he, and he shines with a very great splendor.
Oh Lord, he signifies us to Thee!
Praised be my Lord for our sister the Moon,
and for the stars,
the which He has set clear and lovely in the heaven.
Praised be my Lord for our brother the Wind,
and for air and clouds, calms and all weather,
by which Thou upholdest life and all creatures.
Praised be my Lord for our sister Water,
who is very serviceable to us,
and humble and precious and clean.
Praised be my Lord for our brother Fire,

through whom Thou givest us light in the darkness;
and he is bright and pleasant and very mighty and strong.
Praised be my Lord for our mother the Earth,
the which doth sustain us and keep us,
and bringeth forth divers fruits and flowers of many colors,
and grass.
Praised be my Lord for all those who pardon one another
for love's sake,
and endure weakness and tribulation:
blessed are they who peacefully shall endure,
for Thou, Oh Most High, will give them a crown.
Praised be my Lord for our sister,
the death of the body, from which no man escapeth.
Woe to him who dieth in mortal sin.
Blessed are those who die in Thy most holy will,
for the second death shall have no power to do them harm.
Praise ye and bless the Lord,
and give thanks to Him and serve him with great humility.

† † † † † † † † †

ST. FRANCIS XAVIER (1506 - 1552)   DECEMBER 3

A Basque, born in Navarre on the northern border of Aragon, the youngest of six children, Francis spent his first nineteen years at home, the next eleven at the University of Paris, and the last sixteen at his work. His mother was a wealthy lady and his father a Doctor of Laws at Bologna and chancellor of Navarre. The family fortune deteriorated when his father died about nine years after Francis was born, but there was some money left for he went to college, paid his tutors, and employed another student as his servant.

While a professor of philosophy at the University of Paris, he met Ignatius Loyola and joined the Society of Jesus. After that he travelled, he preached, and he brought the faith to millions. He is considered the greatest missionary since the time of the Apostles. His sermons were accompanied by miracles. In Japan alone he converted a million souls, raised several people from the dead, healed countless others, and foretold the future.

Personally Francis apparently was not physically attractive, but his infinite charm attracted friends wherever he went. He was said to have the patience of an ant and the humility of a dog.

His travels took him to the greater part of the Far East during his ten years of travels, spending three years and seven months of that time at sea. He died waiting on a small island near Hong Kong for a merchant who had promised to smuggle him into China.

† † † † † † † † †

ST. GENESIUS of Rome (3rd century)   AUGUST 25

Even though there are doubts about details, the legend is that Genesius was the leader of a theatrical group in Rome who, while taking part in the burlesque of a Christian baptism during a performance, was suddenly converted and proclaimed himself a believer. The Emperor Diocletian was in the audience enjoying the play but, after finding that Genesius was sincere, had him arrested, tortured, and beheaded.

† † † † † † † † † †

ST. GENEVIEVE (422 - 512)   JANUARY 3

Genevieve was the daugher of Severus and Gerontia, who were either poor peasants or wealthy townspeople, depending on which source one wishes to accept. When she was about seven years old, St. Germain stopped at the small village where she lived, and Genevieve's demeanor and thoughtfulness attracted his attention. After the services he spoke with her and her parents and learned that she was anxious to devote herself to the service of God. He encouraged her in her ambition and when she was fifteen, she formally received the religious veil.

On the death of her parents, Genevieve moved to Paris to live with her godmother. There she did charity work, ate no meat, and broke her fast only twice a week. She was favored with extraordinary gifts, including the ability to read consciences, communicate with the other world, and see the future.

Her prayers were given credit for defeating Attila the Hun who, in 451, was sweeping down upon Gaul, threatening Paris. Genevieve encouraged the people to defend the city, telling them that to flee would be futile and that Paris would be preserved. Events justified her prediction, for the Huns abandoned the road toward Paris and turned toward Orleans where they were defeated by the Romans and the Franks on the Catalonian fields.

† † † † † † † † † †

ST. GEORGE the Great (3rd century) APRIL 23

While it is agreed that George lived and died a martyr, he is one of those "whose actions are only known to God" according to most authorities, including the legend of George's slaying of the dragon.

The legend says that a terrible dragon lived in a lake near the city of Selena in Libya, ravaging all the countryside and threatening the village itself. To keep the dragon at bay, the people gave the dragon two sheep to eat each day. But when sheep became scarce, a human sacrifice became necessary so lots were drawn for a young maiden to be fed to the dragon. On the day St. George rode through the area, the chosen maiden was the daughter of the king. He took pity on the girl and the people of the village so he stayed and, when the dragon appeared, he made the sign of the cross and bravely met the monster who was approaching with open mouth. He killed it with a single blow of his lance.

George then made a speech to the grateful and unafraid townsfolk, and twenty thousand of them were converted. The king offered George half his kingdom, but the saint replied that he must ride on, asking only that the king henceforth should keep the faith and have pity on the needy.

† † † † † † † † †

ST. GERARD MAJELLA (1728 - 1755) OCTOBER 16

Almost since his birth in the small Italian village of Muro, about fifty miles south of Naples, Gerard's only ambition was to be like Jesus in his sufferings and humiliations. When his father died, Gerard had to leave school and become a tailor's apprentice. His earnings were divided into thirds, one third to his mother, another to the poor, and the other portion to the church to have prayers said for the souls in purgatory.

He became a lay brother and his goodness and holiness aroused so much admiration that he was moved from monastery to monastery because of the crowds which constantly surrounded him. He had marvelous and extraordinary gifts, being favored with the ability to read minds, appear to be in two places at once, cure people, tell what was going on somewhere far away, discern spirits, and what seemed to be an unlimited power to control both nature and animals.

A MOTHER'S PRAYER

I call upon thy intercession, Blessed Gerard, before God to bring me boundless love, infinite patience, true understanding, and the strength of character I need to guide my children in their journey through life. I know that the answers and help I need each day will come to me if I ask in thy name with true humility and with firm confidence in thy assistance.

† † † † † † † † †

ST. GERTRUDE of Nivelles (626 - 659)   MARCH 17

Gertrude was the daughter of Blessed Pepin of Landen, and St. Itta, and younger sister of St. Begga. After the death of her father, when she was about thirteen, she and her mother entered a convent. On the family's large properties two monasteries were built, one for men and the other for women. After a visit of some Irish monks who came to evangelize the surrounding countryside, Gertrude gave them a tract of land for their use.

She is specially remembered for her hospitality, and it is believed that if the weather is good on her feast day, crops planted that day will be abundant.

† † † † † † † † †

ST. GILES (7th century)   SEPTEMBER 1

An aristocratic Greek by birth, and a healer by profession, many legends have been woven around the memory of this pious man. Early in life he devoted himself exclusively to spiritual things and his reputation drew multitudes wherever he went. So he withdrew to live as a hermit near the mouth of the Rhone River, and later by the River Gard. His sanctuary was discovered and when the crowds came again, he fled to a dense forest near Nimes, where he spent many years in greatest solitude, with a deer as his sole companion.

† † † † † † † † †

ST. GOMER (717 - 774)   OCTOBER 11

Child of a rich and influential family, Gomer had all the virtues as a child. He was gentle, simple, innocent, and pious. He grew up to be a courageous soldier and to occupy an important position at the court of his relative, King Pepin the Short. The reward for his good service was an arranged marriage with the young, beautiful, and wealthy Gwin Marie.

Possibly at first the marriage was happy, but with Gomer away to fight the wars, Gwin Marie learned to run their estate, look after the family affairs, and rule the employees with an iron fist. She also developed a sharp tongue, a violent temper, a curt manner, and made extravagant demands on all those around her. When Gomer returned home, he tried to undo the damage done to the people on the estate, but there was no peace with Gwin Marie. She only became more bitter and sour-tempered, full of rage and resentment.

So Gomer travelled on pilgrimages, continuing to visit his home only infrequently. However, according to legend, a large number of children were miraculously born to the unhappy couple. When Gwin Marie was near death, she sent for Gomer and he returned to her. He treated her with such compassion, concern, and tenderness that all her spite and viciousness disappeared and she died peacefully.

† † † † † † † † † †

HOLY INNOCENTS (1st century)   DECEMBER 28

These were the male children who were slaughtered in or near Bethlehem by King Herod's order in hopes that the true Messiah would be among them.

This is recorded in Matthew 2, particularly Verse 16. "Then Herod ... was exceeding wroth, and sent forth, and slew all the children that were in Bethlehem, and in all the coasts thereof, from two years old and under ..."

These innocent babies are honored as the first who died for Christ.

† † † † † † † † † †

HOLY ROSARY of Our Lady   OCTOBER 7

It was to St. Dominic that Our Lady appeared in the year 1214, gave him the Holy Rosary, and taught him how to use it.

The rosary is composed of two parts, mental prayer and vocal prayer. While primarily a Roman Catholic ritual, the term has been extended to Muslim, Hindu, and Buddhist prayers that use beads.

The Catholic rosary is a series of fifteen meditations on events, called mysteries, in the lives of Jesus and Mary. They are divided into three groups of five each.

The Joyful Mysteries:
    1—The Annunciation of the Blessed Virgin
    2—The Visitation of the Blessed Virgin to St. Elizabeth
    3—The Birth of Jesus at Bethlehem
    4—The Presentation of Jesus in the Temple
    5—The Finding of the Child Jesus in the Temple

The Sorrowful Mysteries:
    1—The Agony in the Garden of Gethsemane
    2—The Scourging of Jesus at the Pillar
    3—The Crowning of Jesus with Thorns
    4—The Carrying of the Cross by Jesus to Mount Calvary
    5—The Crucifixion of Jesus on Mount Calvary

The Glorious Mysteries:
    1—The Resurrection of Jesus
    2—The Ascension of Jesus
    3—The Descent of the Holy Ghost on the Apostles
    4—The Assumption of the Blessed Virgin into Heaven
    5—The Crowning of the Blessed Virgin in Heaven

Each part consists of one Our Father, ten Hail Marys, and one Glory Be to the Father. Any other prayers of one's own choice are not part of the Rosary, and these added meditations are said before or after each decade—a decade is one set of ten beads.

To begin the Rosary, hold the crucifix in the hand and repeat the Apostle's Creed. Continue to the first bead and say the Our Father. Proceed to the group of three beads and, at each one, repeat the Hail Mary. At the next bead, recite the Glory Be to the Father. This concludes the introductory part of the Rosary.

Proceed past the medallion to the first set of ten beads. Mention one of the Mysteries, and at this point one's own intention may be offered. The prayers then begin. Pray one Our Father. Then on each of the group of ten beads, say the Hail Mary. On the bead which divides the groups of ten beads, repeat the Glory Be to the Father as an ending for the first Mystery, and the Our Father as the beginning for the next Mystery.

Continue in this manner four more times, until the five groups of ten beads have been completed. The fifth Mystery is ended with the final Glory Be to the Father.

The prevalent custom is to say the Joyful Mysteries on Monday and Thursdays and during Advent—the Sunday nearest to the feast of St. Andrew the Apostle which is November 30, and embracing four Sundays. Pray the Sorrowful Mysteries on Tuesdays and Fridays and during Lent—the forty days preceeding Easter. And the Glorious Mysteries on Wednesdays, Saturdays, and Sundays all year round.

Countless blessings can come from the Holy Rosary—grace in abundance during one's lifetime, peace at death, and glory in eternity. Sinners are forgiven, souls that thirst are refreshed, those who are fettered have their bonds broken, those who weep find happiness and joy, those who are tempted find courage, the poor find assistance, those who are ignorant are instructed, the living learn to overcome pride, and the dead have their pains eased by prayers of intercession.

† † † † † † † † †

ST. HUBERT (656 - 728)   NOVEMBER

The eldest son of Bertrand, Duke of Aquitaine, Hubert's youth was spent pursuing worldly comforts and pleasures. At court his charming manners and delightful conversation won him much popularity and he was awarded the dignity of "count of the palace."

His chief passion was hunting and, on Good Friday morning when the faithful were crowding the churches, Hubert sallied forth to the chase. As he pursued a magnificent stag, the animal turned and Hubert was astounded at seeing a crucifix between its antlers. A voice spoke to him, saying "Hubert, unless thou turnest to the Lord and leadest a holy life, thou shalt quickly go down into hell." His conversion was immediate and genuine.

He soon distributed all his wealth to the poor, and began his studies for the priesthood. He travelled widely, burned idols, built sanctuaries, and preached everywhere. Prisoners were especially dear to him and he carried food to them secretly, passing it through the windows of their dungeons.

† † † † † † † † †

ST. IRENE (4th century)   APRIL 3

Irene and her two sisters, Agape and Chionia, were three young maidens brought before the governor of Macedonia, Dulcitius, on a charge of refusing to eat food which had been offered in sacrifice to the pagan gods. When they admitted they were Christians and did not wish to partake of the profane food, Agape and Chionia were burned alive.

Meanwhile Dulcitius had learned that Irene had books of scripture which she had hidden when the emperor's decree against Christians was issued. For this, he ordered her stripped naked and taken to a brothel. But there she remained unmolested, so she was sentenced to death.

† † † † † † † † † †

ST. ISABEL of Portugal (1272 - 1336)   JULY 8

Sometimes called St. Elizabeth, she was the daughter of King Peter II of Spain, and was married at age twelve to King Denis of Portugal. They had two children, Alphonso and Constance.

While her husband was a strong and effective ruler, he was a dreadful husband, and Isabel suffered greatly from his neglect and infidelities. However, she showed no bitterness over his unfaithfulness, carrying her heroism to the extent of bringing up and loving the king's illegitimate children.

Both among her royal relatives, and later, when her son, King Alfonso IV, went to war with Alfonso XI of Castille, Elizabeth served as an effective peacemaker. She is credited with averting or stopping at least five armed conflicts between Spain and Portugal. The task of mediator and reconciler took its toll on her health and she died before she could return home after her final journey to the battlefield.

† † † † † † † † † †

ST. IVES (1253 - 1303)   MAY 19

Born in Brittany as Ivo Helory, he studied in Paris and Orleans, after which he practiced law in both church and civil courts. He defended the poor and unprotected, as well as the rich and influential, and became famous for his fairness, humility, and generosity.

There was a well-known little verse about him, which translates roughly to,

St. Ives was a Breton
A lawyer, not a thief,
and that is a remarkable thing
everyone can see.

In his personal life, Ives lived simply, dressing in coarse burlap. He was poor but joyful, always caring for the unfortunate, and supporting as many as seven orphans in his family home.

† † † † † † † † †

ST. JEAN-BAPTISTE de La Salle (1651 - 1719)   MAY 15

Born at Rheims of an aristocratic family, he became a priest at the age of twenty one, and gave up his life of ease to dedicate himself to the education of the poor. He gave away his considerable fortune and set about opening schools. Jean-Baptiste was the first to establish colleges especially for the training of teachers and sought to inspire his teachers with "a father's love for their pupils, ready to devote all their time and energies to them, as concerned to save them from wickedness as to dispel their ignorance."

His faith, while sometimes shaken, never deserted him. He was a dedicated worker, suffering innumerable persecutions, and died on Good Friday, uttering these last words, "I give thanks to God for all that he has done for me."

† † † † † † † † †

ST. JEROME (342 - 420)   SEPTEMBER 30

Eusebius Hieronymus Sophronius was born of a rich and Christian family. He became one of the most learned men of his era and was among the greatest Biblical scholars. He studied in Rome, particularly the classics. In his youth he was a passionate gambler, especially with dice.

Baptized when he was twenty three, he studied in Rome, and lived as a hermit in Palestine, returning to Rome where he joined the Roman clergy and became secretary to the pope. After being falsely accused of impure relations with a group of upper class ladies, he left Rome, returned to Palestine, and then settled in Bethlehem where he spent his last years in study and translating the Bible.

† † † † † † † † †

ST. JOB (unknown dates)   MAY 10

As the hero of a folk tale, Job was a man who was simple, upright, feared God, and avoided evil. He withstood every test put upon him with dignity and patience and he was rewarded by the Lord's blessings of increased wealth, a long life, and the knowledge that the pure in heart can endure any sufferings.

† † † † † † † † †

ST. JOHN, Apostle and Evangelist (1st century)   DECEMBER 27

The son of Salome and Zebedee, John and his brother, James, were called from their fishing nets by Christ to be apostles. Apparently the brothers were hotheaded and quick tempered for Jesus referred to them as the "sons of thunder." On the other hand their good qualities must have far overshadowed their faults for he chose them to be with him on his transfiguration and his agony in Gethsemane. Tradition has always identified the unnamed disciple "whom Jesus loved" as John, and it was to John that Jesus gave the care of his mother, the Virgin Mary, when he was crucified on the cross. And John was the first to recognize the risen Lord by the Sea of Tiberias.

Of all the sacred writers it is John alone who declares that "God is love." St. Jerome later wrote that, after John was too old to preach, he would simply say to the people who had come to hear him, "Love one another. That is the Lord's command, and if you keep it, that by itself is enough."

PRAYER FOR FAITH

O glorious Apostle, Saint John, I implore thee to set me on fire with a burning love of God. Obtain for me, I pray, this grace from God which will enrich my life here on earth and make me worthy to be united with God forever in heaven.

† † † † † † † † †

ST. JOHN THE BAPTIST (1st century)   JUNE 24

The late born son of the aged priest Zacharias and his wife Elizabeth was given the name John on the explicit orders of the Archangel Gabriel.

John was the immediate forerunner of Jesus, who about the year 27 AD went about as an itinerant preacher, announcing, "Repent, for the Kingdom of Heaven is at hand." He gained many followers, including several who were to become Christ's chosen apostles. John never laid claim to any divine prophesy or special vision and if he performed any miracles, they went unrecorded.

Unlike other saints, St. John's feast day is commemorated on the day of his birth, rather than the day of death. It is one of the oldest feast days, having been celebrated continuously since the fifth century. Many think of Midsummer Day, an anniversary so close to the true summer solstice, as the day on which the year reaches its greatest strength and glory, and thereafter beginning to decline. John's feast day, June 24, is near the time the days begin to grow shorter, while six months later, on Christ's birthday, they begin to increase once again. There is a second St. John's day on August 29, the day of his death by beheading at the hands of Herod, but June 24th is the essential feast day.

† † † † † † † † †

ST. JOHN of God (1495 - 1550)   MARCH 8

Born John Ciudad in Portugal, his parents died when he was quite young. He travelled a while, entered military service, and followed various vocations, including shepherd, peddler, superintendent of slaves, seller of religious books and pictures, and estate manager. He was apparently guilty of many sexual excesses and other grievous sins.

When he was about forty years old, he heard a sermon by St. John of Avila, and was converted with such passion for his new faith that he publicly announced his past sins in such a fervent manner that he was confined to an insane asylum for several months. St. John of Avila visited and convinced him to desist from his public penance and devote his energies into something more helpful to himself and to others. John started on his new path immediately by caring for the other inmates.

The rest of his life was devoted to giving shelter and care to those in need. He rented a house where he could care for the abandoned sick, and miracles happened. Helpers came, people contributed, and his work flourished. He assisted all who came, including vagabonds and prostitutes and when questioned as to why he sheltered tramps and women of bad character, John said only that "the Son of God came for sinners . . ."

† † † † † † † † † †

ST. JOSEPH (1st century)   MARCH 19

Very little is known of Joseph, husband of the Virgin Mary, and foster father of Jesus, except that he was an upstanding man, descendant of the house of David, and a carpenter by profession. Apparently Joseph had died before the crucifixion of Jesus. This is assumed because Jesus would not have commended his mother to John if Joseph had been there to care for her.

Of Joseph's powers of intercession, St. Teresa of Avila said, "I cannot call to mind that I have ever asked him at any time for anything which he has not granted. To other saints our Lord seems to have given grace to help in some special necessity; but to this glorious saint, I know by experience, he has been given grace to help us in all."

PRAYER FOR PURITY

Blessed Saint Joseph, father and guardian of virgins, into whose faithful keeping were entrusted innocency itself, Christ Jesus, and Mary, the Virgin of virgins, I pray and beseech thee to keep me from all uncleanness, and to grant that my mind may be untainted, my heart pure, and my body chaste. Help me always to serve God in perfect chastity.

PRAYER FOR WORKERS

O Glorious St. Joseph, model of all who labor,
obtain for me the grace to work conscientiously,
placing love of duty before frivolous inclinations;
to gratefully work to develop the gifts received from God,
to work methodically, peacefully, in moderation and patience.
Let me not shrink from difficult work for it is through
struggle that unused talents are developed.
Let me do my tasks well, with my best efforts,
And permit me not to be vain in my success.
To imitate thee shall be my desire for life and eternity.

† † † † † † † † † †

49

ST. JULIAN the Hospitaller (Unknown dates)   FEBRUARY 12

Julian, also called The Poor Man, is a folk hero only and the legend is that he was a nobleman who, through a case of mistaken identity, killed his own mother and father in the belief they were burglars who had come into his home. In penance for his crime, he and his wife moved to live by a shallow section of the river where they tended the poor and sick, and ferried travellers across the stream.

✝ ✝ ✝ ✝ ✝ ✝ ✝ ✝ ✝

ST. JUDE (1st century)   OCTOBER 28

One of the apostles, also called Thaddaeus, and brother of James the Less. He is believed to be the author of the book of Jude in the New Testament, but this is not altogether certain.

He preached in Persia and was martyred there with his fellow apostle Simon.

St. Jude is possibly the most popular of all saints for he is known as the Saint of the Impossible and is used for what seems to be hopeless causes.

PRAYER FOR A DESPERATE SITUATION

O God, through your Blessed St. Jude, I pray for help in my extreme need. The despair I feel has blocked out all hope, all confidence, all faith in a just solution to this situation. Bring to me a spirit of trust and an optimistic attitude which will bring about an improvement of my circumstances. Thou knowest my needs and I pray for speedy assistance, along with a restoration of my knowledge that all things work for good when trust in your mercy is placed above all other thoughts.

✝ ✝ ✝ ✝ ✝ ✝ ✝ ✝ ✝

ST. LAWRENCE (3rd century)   AUGUST 10

At the beginning of the month of August, 258, the emperor Valerian issued an order that all bishops, deacons, and priests were to be put to death. Pope Sixtus II was found and executed, and the persecutors came to claim the church's possessions. Deacon

50

Lawrence was arrested, but asked for three days to get together and inventory the treasures at his command. The time was granted, and he used it to turn all goods into cash and distribute the money to the needy. On the fourth day, Lawrence came back, followed by a crowd of widows, orphans, lepers, beggars, cripples, children, and old people. "Behold the treasures of the church" he told the judge who then condemned him to death by burning in the belief that the torture would make him reveal where the treasures were hidden. Instead, Lawrence showed not only remarkable courage but admirable humor. After the fire started, he told his tormentors, "My flesh is well cooked on one side, turn the other, and eat," dying with his eyes toward heaven.

PRAYER FOR FORTITUDE
O Glorious St. Lawrence, who did not lose thy faith when being subjected to the most bitter torments, obtain for me this active and solid conviction of God's love, justice, and mercy so that I may also withstand the trials which beset me.

† † † † † † † † †

ST. LEONARD (unknown date)   NOVEMBER 6
Nothing certain is known, but according to legend Leonard belonged to a noble French family during the reign of King Clovis. He obtained from the king the release of a great number of prisoners. Later he entered a monastery and went to Aquitaine to preach. Through his prayers the Queen of the Franks survived a difficult confinement and was delivered of a healthy child.

In the 12th century numerous manacles and chains could be seen along the highways hanging on stone crosses. These were left in homage to Leonard who had assisted in getting them freed.

† † † † † † † † †

ST. LOUIS of France (1215 - 1270)   AUGUST 25
Louis became king at the age of eleven, married Marguerite of Provence at nineteen by whom he had eleven children, six sons and five daughters. His mother was Blanche of Castile, a pious domineering woman who told her son, "I had rather see you dead at my feet than guilty of a mortal sin."

He was a man of sound common sense, possessing indefatigable energy, graciously kind, and of playful humor, constantly guarding against the temptation to be arrogant, proving that he apparently took note of his mother's admonition.

When Louis took office, the death penalty was applied to murder, arson, rape, treason, highway robbery, horse theft, complicity in a crime of any kind, escape from prison, and possession of an animal which caused the death of another. Under his rule, justice was tempered with mercy and, through his personal qualities as well as his saintliness, increased for many years the prestige of the French monarchy.

He led two crusades, the first to Egypt where he was taken prisoner. During the second he died of typhus near Tunis.

Two of the maxims attributed to him are these. "No possession is joyous without a companion" and "Do not contradict anyone unless silence would be sinful."

† † † † † † † † †

ST. LUCY (3rd century)   DECEMBER 13

According to the traditional story, Lucy was born of rich and noble parents about the year 283. Her father was Roman and her mother's name was Eutychia, which seems to indicate that she came of Greek stock.

Lucy had early consecrated herself to God and hoped to use her worldly goods to serve the poor. Her mother was not so high minded but, after a pilgrimage made to the relics of St. Agatha where Eutychia was cured of hemorrages from which she had suffered for several years, Lucy persuaded her mother to allow a great part of their riches to be distributed among the needy.

The giving away of some of her fortune angered a young nobleman to whom Lucy has been engaged for three years, and he denounced her to the Governor of Sicily. This was in the year 303, during the fierce persecution of Diocletian. Lucy was condemned to a house of prostitution, but she could not be forced to leave the court, an invincible force keeping her rooted to the spot. Even a yoke of oxen could not drag her to the place of shame. Finally a pyre was lighted about her, but even then she remained alive in the midst of flames so an executioner pierced her throat with his dagger.

PRAYER FOR A DREAM TO SEE A FUTURE HUSBAND
Sweet St. Lucy, let me know
Whose cloth I shall lay,
Whose bed I shall make,
Whose child I shall bear,
Whose darling I shall be,
Whose arms I shall lie in.

† † † † † † † † †

ST. LUKE (1st century)   OCTOBER 18
The only one of the apostles who was not a Jew, Luke was a Greek born in Antioch, Syria, and a physician by profession. He became a worker with St. Paul and stayed with him until Paul's death.

Luke was a man of sensitivity and compassion, with sympathy to the role of women and minorities. His leniency and sympathy for sinners is expressed in some of the most poignant parables which he alone recorded, including the incident of the sinful woman kissing Christ's feet, and the stories of the good thief and the prodigal son.

Nothing is known of his later life except that he died when he was about eighty five, unmarried and childless.

† † † † † † † † †

ST. MARGARET (3rd century)   JULY 20
Also called Marina, she was the daughter of a pagan priest. Her mother died soon after her birth, and she was nursed by a pious woman nearby. A Roman official was attracted by her great beauty when he saw her watching the flocks of her mistress one day, and sought to make her his paramour or his wife. When neither flattery nor threats of punishment could persuade her to yield to his desires, he had her brought to public trial at Antioch.

Threatened with death unless she renounced her faith and paid homage to the pagan gods, she refused and was condemned to the stake. An attempt was made to burn her, but the flames flickered and died, leaving her unhurt. She was then bound hand and foot and thrown into a cauldron of boiling water, but her bonds were loosened and she stood up uninjured. She was thrown into a dungeon where a terrible dragon came and swallowed her, at which time the dragon died on the spot, and Margaret came out alive and undamaged. Finally she was beheaded.

† † † † † † † † †

ST. MARTHA (1st century)   JULY 29

Martha was the sister of Lazarus and Mary, and probably the eldest of the three. It was she who was hostess to Jesus when he visited their home at Bethany, a small town just outside of Jerusalem. Martha typifies the active life for, when Jesus visited, it was Martha who did the serving while Mary sat listening to the visitor speak. And, when Martha complained, Jesus told her that each person had a place in life and comparisons between the worthiness of each one's role should not be made.

It is legendary only that later in life Martha lived in France and taught in the Rhone Valley. A dragon appeared out of the river, wreaking havoc, burning with its breath, and trampling everything in its path. Martha sprinkled it with holy water, tied it with her garter, and led it meekly to the slaughter.

PRAYER FOR NECESSITIES

Saint Martha, I come for thy aid and protection. Comfort me in all my difficulties, and through the great favors thou didst enjoy when the Saviour was lodged in thy house, intercede for my family that we may be provided for in our necessities. I ask of thee, Saint Martha, to obtain for us the grace to overcome all obstacles which confront us.

† † † † † † † † †

ST. MARTIN de Porres (1579 - 1639)   NOVEMBER 3

Martin was a mulatto, natural son of John de Porres, a Spanish nobleman, and Anna Velasquez, a black dancer from Panama. His father refused to acknowledge him until he was about twelve, after which Martin was provided with an education. Up until that time he shared an impoverished life with his unmarried mother.

Martin became a lay brother and spent his life serving as barber, farm laborer, in the infirmary, wherever he was needed. He was devoted to the sick, to caring for beggars, and had a great concern for animals, including rats and other vermin. He was a one man humane society, keeping a hospital for dogs and cats at his sister's home.

Martin's humility inspired everyone with whom he came in contact. He forgave the faults of others, excused the bitterest injuries, lovingly comforted the sick, and helped the needy as best he could.

PRAYER FOR ASSISTANCE

Most humble Martin de Porres, whose burning charity embraced not only the needy brethren but also the very animals of the field, we hail and invoke thee. Blessed Martin, who always had sympathy for the poor and suffering, I need your help, and ask it now with great confidence in your goodness and power. This is the problem I place in your care ———————— (state the situation).

† † † † † † † † †

ST. MARTIN of Tours (316 - 387)   NOVEMBER 11

Born in what is now Hungary and educated in Italy, Martin was the son of pagan parents. His father was a Roman army officer and, at the age of fifteen, Martin was forced to serve in the army. After becoming a Christian, he lived more like a monk than a soldier, and became perhaps the first "conscientious objector." He was twenty three when he refused to continue as a soldier, saying "I am a soldier of Christ and it is not lawful for me to fight."

A famous legend about Martin says that, while still a soldier, he met a beggar who was almost naked. It was a bitterly cold day so Martin took his own cloak from around his shoulders, cut it in half, and gave one part to the man. That night in his sleep Christ appeared to Martin dressed in the half of the garment and said, "Martin has covered me this day."

Martin was often plagued by the devil who came to him in varying forms— sometimes as gods or goddesses of pagan mythology. Mercury, Jupiter, Venus, or Minerva would appear to tempt him, but he drove them away with prayer and the sign of the cross.

PRAYER AGAINST IMPURE THOUGHTS

With trust and faith I beg thee, Blessed St. Martin, to defend me against impure and evil thoughts which may stain my soul and come between my desire for the true and complete satisfaction which is offered through perfect love. Rescue me from the mire lest I sink. Let not the deep swallow me up. Thy mercy is great, draw near to me and lift me up, I pray.

† † † † † † † † †

MARY, The Blessed Virgin (1st century) AUGUST 15

The mother of Jesus was a Jewish maiden, traditionally of the family of King David. The place of her birth is unknown. In Hebrew she was called Miriam.

Mary was engaged to marry Joseph when an angel came to her, announcing that the Holy Spirit would come upon her and that by his power she would bear a son to be known as the Son of God.

After Christ's ascension, Mary was with the apostles and the others, watching and praying in the upper room until they were filled with the Holy Spirit at Pentecost. This is the last reference to Mary in the scripture, and nothing whatever is known of the rest of her life, not even where or when she died.

That Mary was the virgin mother of Christ is made plain in the Bible, and Christians believe that she remained a virgin throughout her life. In some faiths, it is believed that Mary was preserved from "original sin" from the moment of her conception in her mother's womb, the "immaculate conception." Also, without denying that she died a natural death, it is believed that at the end of her earthly life, Mary was taken to heaven in both soul and body, her "assumption."

PRAYER WHEN IN NEED

Blessed Mary, Mother of God, in my hour of need I call upon you. Look down upon the sick and suffering and enfold them in your love. Bring thy help in turning illness into health, replacing pain with blessed relief, change defeat into victory, darkness into light, discouragement into hope, sorrow into joy, and displace despondency with the knowledge that you are the strength of the weak and the comforter of the distressed.

DAILY PRAYER TO MARY

All fair art thou, O Mary!
The original stain is not in thee.
Thou art the glory of Jerusalem.
Thou art the joy of Israel.
Thou art the honor of our people.
Thou art the advocate of sinners.
O Mary, Virgin most prudent.
Mother most tender, pray for us.
Intercede for us with our Lord Jesus Christ.
In thy conception, Virgin, thou wast immaculate.

Pray for us to the Father, whose Son was born of thee.

† † † † † † † † †

ST. MARY MAGDALENE (1st century)   JULY 22

Mary Magdalene's identity will always remain a mystery. Was she the unnamed sinful woman who annointed the feet of Jesus? Was she the one who Jesus delivered from evil spirits? Was she the sister of Martha and Lazarus? It does not matter for, even if she were the harlot who came to kneel before Christ, anointing his feet with kisses, tears, and perfume, then drying them with her hair, Jesus raised her up and said, "Thy faith has saved thee, go in peace."

Mary Magdalene's story only proves that, no matter how lurid the past has been, or how many sins have been commited, the saving power of faith is available for those who chose it.

PRAYER FOR PATIENCE

Blessed Mary Magdalene, help me to remain quiet in my trials and submit to God's will for me. I know that my tolerance is lacking, my hands are tired, and my spirit is listless. Have mercy on my weakness. Strengthen my desire to hold my peace with the knowledge that, with your help, I can truly come to say, "Father, not my will, but Thine, be done."

PRAYER FOR SELF-IMPROVEMENT

Dear Mary Magdalene, take away my faults of character which cause me to be sullen, selfish, and introverted. Let me turn my thoughts and affection outward toward others—thoughts of kindness, concern, caring, and passion. Help me to mold myself in thy image, that I may be able to freely and completely give and receive love. I know that I must love others in order to be loved and I beg thy help in my efforts to forget myself, keeping my attentions directed toward those I encounter.

† † † † † † † † †

ST. MATTHIAS (1st century)   FEBRUARY 24

Matthias was with Jesus from baptism to the ascension and, after the ascension, an assembly of over a hundred of Christ's followers met together. There Peter proposed that a disciple be chosen to fill the place of the traitor Judas Iscariot among the Twelve Apostles. When lots were drawn, the choice fell to Matthias.

All further information about his life and death are vague and contradictory. Some say he preached in Judea and Ethiopia, and then was crucified. Another source says he was stoned at Jerusalem by the Jews and beheaded there. Yet another tells of his mission to the interior of Ethopia where he preached to the barbarians and cannibals, his death at Sebastopolis, and his burial near the Temple of the Sun.

PRAYER FOR AN ALCOHOLIC

Gracious Saint Matthias, the helper of all who put their trust in thee, we pray for all those enslaved by intoxicants, and especially for —————— (state name). Give this one the desire and the will to be free, and the grace to continue in the path toward abstinence. I ask thy help in confidence that you can bring freedom to those bound by the chains of addiction.

† † † † † † † † † †

ST. MAURICE (3rd century)   SEPTEMBER 22

Maurice was leader of the Theban Legion, composed entirely of Christians, in the army of Maximian Herculius. They had been called from Africa to suppress a revolt in Gaul. While camped in Switzerland the soldiers were ordered to sacrifice to the gods in thanksgiving and in preparation for the upcoming battle.

The entire legion of 6,600 men refused to participate in the pagan rites and, as a result, were massacred en masse.

† † † † † † † † † †

ST. MICHAEL the Archangle (unknown date)   SEPTEMBER 29

St. Michael is, with Sts. Gabriel and Raphael, one of the three archangels mentioned in scripture. He is highest in rank of the seven principal angels, having four principal obligations. These are to fight against Satan, to rescue souls from the power of the devil, to champion all God's people, and to call away from earth and bring the souls of the dead to judgment.

PRAYER FOR VICTORY IN BATTLE

St. Michael the Archangel, defend us in battle.
Be our protection against the wickedness and snares of the devil.
May God rebuke him, we humbly pray.
And do thou, O prince of the heavenly host,

By the power of God,
Thrust into hell Satan and all evil spirits
Who wander through the world for the ruin of souls.

PRAYER FOR DELIVERANCE FROM ENEMIES
St. Michael, thy help is my salvation. I ask thee to guard me from danger, deliver me from all evil. Free my enemies from the bondage of hatred, and let not anger burn in their hearts. Instill in them the peace and love and forgiveness toward me which I bear toward them. Let me by my example prove my sincerity in my efforts to turn from rage and wrath, inviting in its place love and tranquility.

† † † † † † † † †

ST. NICHOLAS (died 350)   DECEMBER 6
One of the most popular of all saints for he has evolved into Father Christmas, or Santa Claus, of recent times. Almost nothing factual is known about his life, except that he was Bishop of Myra in the fourth century. However, legends abound to supply details of Nicholas as an ardent apostle and preacher of truth, known for his generosity, care of the young, and innumerable miracles.

One of his miracles was the raising from the dead three children who had been pickled in a salting tub.

Another tale is that of a poor man who had three daughters who received no offers of marriage because they had no dowry. The father was desperate and had almost decided to send them to a brothel. But Nicholas went to the house one evening, threw into an open window a purse filled with gold, and a few days later, the eldest daughter was married. A while later, Nicholas delivered a second dowry and the middle daughter found a husband. On his third visit, the father was waiting in hiding and recognized Nicholas. He fell weeping in penitence of his previous intention to send the girls to the disorderly house, and from then on sang the praises of the good St. Nicholas everywhere.

Twice Nicholas came to the rescue of three innocent men who were unjustly accused and condemned to death. He went to the prison, forced the guards to release the prisoners, and then confronted the governor who had been bribed to accuse the men. The governor acknowledged his wrongdoing in the presence of three officers who were passing through. Later, these three were also accused and condemned, but Nicholas miraculously freed them.

† † † † † † † † †

ST. NOTBURGA (1265 - 1313)   SEPTEMBER 13

A peasant's daughter, Notburga was employed as cook and kitchen maid at the castle of Count Henry of Rothenburg. She was an awkward girl, fat, and with a squint. Some say she only had one eye. In spite of her unattractive physical appearance, her spirit was beautiful. She fulfilled her humble duties joyfully and gave food to the poor when she had been told to feed it to the pigs. Ottilia, her mistress, dismissed her when her charity to the needy was discovered, but shortly thereafter, Ottilia fell ill and Notburga returned to care for her.

On an occasion when Notburga was asked to reap corn on the Sabbath, rather than attend church as was her custom, she refused. When urged by her master to continue, she threw her sickle in the air, saying, "Let my sickle be judge between me and you," and it remained suspended out of reach.

† † † † † † † † †

ST. ODILIA (7th century)   DECEMBER 13

Odilia's father, Adalric, Duke of Alsace, had hoped for a son to perpetuate the family name, but a blind daughter was born. He wanted to kill the baby but her mother, Beresinde, saved her by sending her to a wet nurse who lived a few miles away.

At the age of twelve, Odilia was baptized and instantaneously recovered her sight. After that, she and her father were reconciled and she returned home. He wanted her to marry, but she refused as she wished to become a nun. He accepted her decision and gave her a fine castle which she converted into a convent.

† † † † † † † † †

ST. ODO of Cluny (879 - 942)   NOVEMBER 18

Odo spent several years at the court of William, Duke of Aquitaine, and when he was about thirty years old, became a monk, priest, and head of an abbey school. He studied music and poetry, and pursued these interests all of his life. He established schools which attracted people of distinction and influence.

Lost in obscurity is the reason for his power to bring rain when asked.

✝ ✝ ✝ ✝ ✝ ✝ ✝ ✝ ✝

ST. PANTALEON (3rd century)   JULY 27
Son of a rich pagan, Eustorgius of Nicomedia, and a Christian mother, Eubula, Pantaleon studied medicine and became physician to the Emperor Maximianus. When his father died, he came into a large fortune and envious colleagues denounced him to the emperor during the Diocletian persecutions.

Even though he healed a paralytic as proof that Christ is the true God, he was condemned to death. First his flesh was burned with torches, but their flames were extinguished. A bath of hot lead was prepared but when he stepped in, the lead became cold. He was thrown into the sea with a stone about his neck, but the stone floated. He was thrown to the wild beasts, but they would not attack. Bound to the wheel, the ropes snapped and the wheel broke. An attempt was made to behead him, but the sword bent and his executioner was converted. Pantaleon implored heaven to forgive his tormentors which earned him the title of the "all compassionate." It was not until he himself desired it that it was possible for the sword to decapitate him.

✝ ✝ ✝ ✝ ✝ ✝ ✝ ✝ ✝

ST. PATRICK (387 - 493)   MARCH 17
Born a Briton, with Ireland, Scotland, and Wales all claiming to have been his birthplace, Patrick was carried off by raiders when he was about sixteen years old. He was taken as a captive to Ireland and there he was used as a herdsman. After six years he made his escape, but once he was back home, he had a dream in which he heard "the voice of the Irish" saying "come and walk among us once more," so about 432 or thereabout he returned to Ireland as a dynamic preacher.

Until his death Patrick founded and watched over churches all over Ireland. At one time he spent forty days on the summit of Eagle Mountain, now known as St. Patrick's Mountain and honored as the

Holy Hill. His purpose was to obtain special blessing and mercy for the Irish, and at length his prayers were heard. Among Patrick's Promises is one which assures the Irish that Patrick himself will be the one who will judge them on last day.

ST. PATRICK'S PRAYER FOR PROTECTION

I bind to myself today
God's power to guide me,
God's might to uphold me,
God's wisdom to teach me,
God's ear to hear me,
God's eye to watch over me,
God's word to give me speech,
God's hand to guard me,
God's way to lie before me,
God's shield to protect me
against the snares of demons,
against the seductions of vices,
against the lusts of nature,
against those who wish me ill.
Christ, protect me today.

† † † † † † † † †

ST. PAUL (1st century)   JUNE 30

Paul was a Roman citizen, born at Tarsus of an important and devout Jewish family. He was highly educated, speaking both Aramaic and Greek, and a student of both Jewish dogma and traditional law. Physically he is believed to have been a man of short stature, less than five feet tall, broad-shouldered, closely-knit eyebrows, fair complexion, a thick greyish beard, and somewhat bald.

In his eye, to worship Christ was to betray the religious ideal of Israel. He persecuted the Christians with zeal until the day the risen Christ appeared to him. From that moment on, he was transformed and wholly devoted to spreading the love of God.

His last years are almost lost in obscurity. It is only possible to establish that he suffered martyrdom near Rome towards the end of the reign of Nero, possibly about the year 65 AD.

PRAYER FOR A HOLY DEATH

O glorious Saint Paul, on earth thou wast a mirror of innocence and a model of penance. Thy life was spent in bringing back the erring souls of countless unfortunate sinners. Do mercifully look down once more from heaven and hear my petition. Obtain for me so great a love of Jesus that I may make His sufferings mine. Let me realize in the wounds of my Saviour the wickedness of my transgressions, and obtain from them, as from the fountain of salvation, the grace of bitter tears and a resolution to imitate thee in thy penance. Finally, intercede for me that I may, by the grace of God, die a holy death, and come at last to enjoy with thee His blessed presence in heaven for all eternity.

PRAYER FOR ACCEPTANCE
O glorious Saint Paul, who did suffer prison, beatings, criticism, stonings, and all manner of persecutions, obtain for us the grace to accept the infirmities, sufferings, and misfortunes of this life with grace and with fortitude, secure in the knowledge that no burden beyond our strength will be placed upon us. Pray for us, Saint Paul the Apostle.

† † † † † † † † † †

ST. PETER (1st century)   JUNE 29
Peter was married, had children, and was a fisherman on the Sea of Galilee when he and his brother, Andrew, were called to follow Christ and be "a fisher of men." At the time his name was Simon, but Jesus gave him the Aramaic title of Keph, meaning "rock" of which the Greek equivalent in English became Peter.

When later Christ chose the twelve apostles, it appears clear that Peter soon became conspicuous among them. In the list of them, Peter stands always first. On various occasions Peter speaks in the names of the other apostles, and frequently Christ turns specially to Peter. Jesus said to him, "Thou art Peter, and upon this rock I will build my church" conferring on him "the keys of the kingdom of Heaven" and the powers of "binding and loosing."

After the ascension, Peter pursued his evangelistic labors, possibly in Asia Minor. He was put to death under Emperor Nero, being crucified with head downward by his own request.

PRAYER FOR STRENGTH
Hear my prayer according to thy faithfulness, answer me according to thy justice. My spirit grows faint and my heart grows numb. I stretch out my arms to thee, asking thy speedy mercy. Show me the way I should go, deliver me from my foes, teach me to do thy will.

Let faithfulness spring from my heart and contentment overpower my spirit so that I may go forth restored by love, confident that all my undertakings which are begun in sincerity will come to a quick and satisfactory conclusion.

PRAYER FOR FORGIVENESS OF SINS

Blessed Apostle Peter, to whom God has given the keys of the kingdom of heaven, and the power to bind and loose; grant that we may be delivered, through the help of intercession, from the bonds of our sins.

† † † † † † † † †

ST. PETER CLAVER (1580 - 1654)   SEPTEMBER 9

A native of Spain, he left his homeland in 1610 to work in the service of blacks for the remainder of his life. On his religious chart, he wrote, "Peter, slave of the slaves forever."

Upon his arrival at Cartegena, now in Columbia, he was met by a slave ship being unloaded. The blacks had been stolen from Africa, hunted down like beasts in the forests and grasslands, and piled into the boats, one on top of another. An estimated one-third of them died en route. Those who survived the voyage were herded out of the ships like chained animals and shut up in nearby yards to be gazed at by the crowds. Peter went among them with medicines, lemons, brandy, biscuits, food, and tobacco.

For forty years he met every ship, followed his blood stained flock to the compounds, gave them strength, nourishment, loyalty, and love. He often said, "We must speak to them with our hands before we try to speak to them with our lips." Peter suffered for four years with ill health and died of the plague. He had ministered to the slaves with his hands and heart, and had baptized nearly 300,000 of them.

† † † † † † † † † † †

ST. QUENTIN (3rd century)   OCTOBER 31

The son of the Roman senator Zenonius, little is known of his life except that he left Rome to preach in the vicinity of Beauvais and Amiens. It was in Amiens that he was imprisoned, tortured, and beheaded.

One legend of St. Quentin's aid is recorded in the story of a thief who was sentenced to death after a priest made a complaint about the crime. The priest was distressed by the severity of the punishment and pleaded with the judge to lessen the punishment. His request was refused, so the priest prayed to St. Quentin to intervene. On the day of the hanging, the condemned man dropped through the trap door of the gallows, but the rope broke. The judge then considered this a sign and set the thief free.

† † † † † † † † †

ST. RAPHAEL (unknown date)   OCTOBER 24

Raphael, one of the seven archangels standing before the throne of God, was sent in human form as the traveling companion of the young Tobias who was on his way to be the eighth husband of Sara, whose seven previous husbands had been slain by a demon. Raphael bound the demon, Asmodeus, "in the desert of upper Egypt." Thus Sara was delivered from the devil and her marriage to Tobias was blessed.

On this same journey Raphael restored sight to Tobias' father who was blind.

Raphael, or "Healer of God," is assumed to be the angel who, as told in John 5:4 "troubled the water" and "whosoever then first after the troubling of the water stepped in was made whole of whatsoever disease he had."

† † † † † † † † †

ST. RAYMOND NONNATUS (1200 - 1240)

Nonnatus is a surname given him because he was delivered by Caesarean operation after his mother's death.

His father encouraged him to get a good education and he was ordained in 1222. He made such progress in the religious life that he was soon considered worthy to take over the office of ransomer. He was sent to Algiers and liberated many Christian captives. When he did not have enough money to ransom some prisoners, he gave himself in exchange. Subjected to all kinds of indignities and cruelty, he was made to run the gauntlet, and then sentenced to impalement. The punishment was commuted in the hope of ransoming Raymond for a greater sum of money. To prevent him preaching about Christ, his lips were pierced with a red-hot iron and closed with a padlock.

Finally money was brought for his release and he returned to Rome where he spent the last ten years of his life, dying of fever when he was about forty years old.

† † † † † † † † †

ST. RITA (1381 - 1457)   MAY 22

The "saint of the impossible" was born to her parents so late in their lives that her birth seemed to be the first miracle of her life. They brought her up in a spirit of holy gratitude and, by the time she was twelve her love for Jesus was so great that she sought to become a nun. But her parents were aging and were worried about Rita being left alone in the world, so they arranged a marriage for her. She became the wife of a brute and a drunkard but Rita's love for him and her prayers brought him to love God. This was regarded as her second unachievable case.

Later her husband was murdered and her sons were determined to avenge their father's death. Rita prayed to turn them from their murderous rage and her prayers were answered. This was her third impossible situation.

Rita then, after much difficulty for only virgins were permitted, miraculously entered a convent of Augustinian nuns and they permitted her to remain. She received the stigmata in the form of a cancerous sore on her forehead, and suffered greatly from it, but was able to cure and comfort many others before her death at the age of seventy three.

† † † † † † † † †

ST. ROCK (1295 - 1327)   AUGUST 16

A rich young Frenchman, son of the governor of Montpellier, Rock distributed his wealth to the poor and turned over the government to an uncle when his father died. He was about twenty years old and determined to care for those stricken by the plague which was running rampant in Italy. Everywhere he went, healing the sick with the sign of the cross, the terrible scourge disappeared before his miraculous power.

66

When he himself was stricken and lay dying of hunger in a forest, Rock was fed by a dog which came every day and brought him a piece of bread stolen from his master's table. Becoming suspicious of the dog which took bread with such regularity, the master one day followed the dog, found the sick man, became Rock's friend, and learned from him a better way of life.

Rock recovered from the plague and returned to his birthplace, but his sufferings had so disfigured him that he was taken for a spy and thrown into a dungeon. He died there and just after his death the jailer, Justin, came into the cell and nudged Rock's body with the leg which had been lame from birth. Miraculously he was cured.

† † † † † † † † †

ST. SCHOLASTICA (480 - 543) FEBRUARY 10

The twin sister of St. Benedict, their mother died in childbirth. The two children were together until they were fourteen when Benedict left for Rome to pursue his studies. Later, when he became a monk and she a nun, they lived in the same area but saw each other only once a year. They would meet in a guest house of the abbey and eat together, after which each would return to his own home.

The last time Scholastica and Benedict met is reported by St. Gregory who writes that supper was finished and it was time for the two to separate. Scholastica asked her brother to stay the night so they could continue their conversation about the joys of Heaven. But Benedict refused, saying that he "not for the world would pass a night outside the monastery." Scholastica wept for a moment in silence, then hid her face in her hands. Only a few moments later a crash of thunder shook the house, the sky became black, flashes of lightning illuminated the night, the wind blew, the skies opened their floodgates, and the storm raged. Benedict's departure was impossible, and Scholastica told Benedict that since he would not do as she asked, she had asked God and he had heard her by sending the storm so that Benedict would be forced to do as she wished. The two spent the night in prayer and conversation and parted at dawn, when the storm quieted, and never saw each other again. It was three days later, as Benedict was at the window of his room, that he saw the soul of his sister rising to heaven in the form of a dove.

† † † † † † † † †

ST. SERVATUS (4th century) MAY 13

Little has been written about his personal life or character. The story of his Jewish origins and his relationship with St. Anne do not appear to be factual.

It is known that he was Bishop of Tongres during a period when Christianity was in turmoil. There were those in the church who had Arian tendencies—the belief that Christ, the Son, is not of the same substance as God, the Father, and, therefore, Jesus was not divine.

The source of his powers is unclear, but he is called upon for protection against mice and rats, and for success in any endeavor.

† † † † † † † † † †

SEVEN SLEEPERS OF EPHESUS (3rd century) JULY 27

There are many versions of this legend of the sleepers who awake many years later to find the world changed, and makes one of the most curious stories about saints who have suffered and died for their faith.

The Emperor Decius came to Ephesus about the year 250 to enforce his laws against Christians. He found seven noble men whose names are not certain, but could have been Achillides, Diomedes, Diogenus, Probatus, Stephanus, Sambatus, and Quiriacus. They refused to offer the required sacrifice to the pagan gods, and having endangered their lives by the refusal, fled to a cavern on Mount Celion. Their hiding place was discovered and the emperor had the cave sealed with stone while the young men were asleep.

Time passed and the men were forgotten. Decius died and others reigned. Eventually the age of persecution of the Christians ceased. It was near the middle of the fifth century when a rich landowner had his workmen move the stones from the sealed cave so that it could be used as a cattle stall.

The sleepers awoke, thinking only a single night had passed while they slept. They left their cave and went to the city and, even though there was no longer any danger of persecution, they encountered many troubles. The shopkeepers would not accept their archaic coins for the purchase of food, and they could not find their way about the city for it had grown and changed during the two hundred years they had been asleep.

Of course, the whole story comes out in time, and the sleepers believed they had been awakened to prove the resurrection of the dead. Everyone rejoices at this confirmation of their faith's doctrine, and the saints die praising God. They were buried again in the cave where they had slept for over two hundred years.

PRAYER FOR THE SLEEPLESS
I pray for rest which is sorely needed. You, Blessed Sleepers of Ephesus, can watch this night and bring to me the security I need to close my eyes and drift into dreamless sleep with the sure knowledge that no harm will come to me or my loved ones while I slumber.

† † † † † † † † † †

ST. SIMON (1st century)   OCTOBER 28
This is Simon the Zealot, signifying that he had zeal for the Jewish law which he practiced before his call to be an Apostle. He was present at the scene of Christ's first miracle, the changing of the water into wine at the wedding in Cana.

Nothing positive can be said about his later life and activities. There are reports of his preaching in such diverse locations as Babylon, Persia, Samaria, Egypt, North Africa, and Britain. Where or how he died, and his place of burial is unknown.

† † † † † † † † † †

ST. STEPHEN (1st century)   DECEMBER 26
Called the first martyr because, except for the Holy Innocents who were the babies slaughtered by King Herod's order in an attempt to kill the young Jesus, Stephen was the first to shed blood for the Christian faith.

Little is known of his life before he was named one of seven deacons chosen to look after the needs of the Greek-speaking widows among the Christians at Jerusalem. His previous life remains obscure, not even when or in what circumstance he became a Christian. By selecting him for a deacon, the church publicly acknowledged him as a man "of good reputation, full of faith and fortitude." He had the gift of superior oratorical powers and unimpeachable logic and he did "great wonders and miracles" along with his sermons. He was denounced to the Jewish council as a blasphemer. He addressed them at length, his wisdom and clear manner of speaking presenting the evidence that Jesus was the messiah announced by Moses and the prophets. But they rejected his message and he was stoned to death. As he was dying, Stephen prayed "Lord, do not count this sin against them."

† † † † † † † † †

ST. TERESA of Avila (1515 - 1582)   OCTOBER 15

The third child of Don Alonso Sanchez de Cepeda by his second wife, Dona Beatriz Davila y Ahumada, Teresa was brought up by her saintly father, a lover of serious books, and a tender and pious mother. Early in life she showed the qualities which would make her special, reading the lives of the saints which led her to enter the religious life.

Teresa entered the convent when she was eighteen and the following year became very seriously ill. Even after a partial recovery through the intercession of St. Joseph, her health remained permanently impaired. Yet despite her frailty she stayed ever active, opening new convents, smoothing difficulties for her nuns, placating those in authority, and all the while being favored with remarkable mystical experiences.

She loved God, children, and her friends all with the same enthusiasm, and once said, "I have no defense against affection. I could be bribed with a sardine." Teresa is the saint of sound common sense, of good humor, of generous ideals, and a talented, attractive, original, and unself-conscious woman. She wrote lovely poetry, and was an inspired executive. When she died, the Duchess of Alva covered her with a cloth of gold—signifying not riches, but nobility.

"Pray in secret" Teresa advised, "and your father will reward you openly."

ST. TERESA'S BOOK-MARK
Let nothing disturb thee;
Let nothing dismay thee;
All things pass:
God never changes.
Patience attains
All that is strived for.

He who has God
Finds he lacks nothing:
God alone suffices.

ST. TERESA'S PRAYER FOR SOLACE

O my Lord,
when I think in how many ways Thou hast suffered,
and that Thou didst in no wise deserve it,
I do not know what to say for myself,
nor of what I am thinking when I shrink from suffering,
nor where I am when I excuse myself.
O Jesus, Thou brightness of eternal glory,
solace of the pilgrim soul,
with Thee is my mouth without voice,
and my silence speaks to Thee.

PRAYER FOR HUMILITY AND SPIRITUALITY

I come to you for help, Blessed Saint Teresa. My vanity, my pride,
and my arrogance are keeping me from knowing the love of God and
of others. Grant me the simplicity which springs directly from
nature and from which true greatness comes. Cause me to be truth-
ful, resisting all temptations to falsify or indulge in exaggerations.
Take from me the base instincts which cause me to wander from my
goal which is to be at peace with all people, and to know God in my
daily life.

† † † † † † † † †

ST. THERESA of Lisieux (1873 - 1897)　　　　OCTOBER 3

Called the Little Flower of Jesus, Marie Francoise Theresa
Martin was born at Alencon, and entered the Carmelite Order at the
age of fifteen. A dutiful daughter, thoughtful pupil, gentle sister,
lover of laughter and of God, Theresa's short life was remarkable for
its simplicity, humility, and courage. She showed her love of God by
love of neighbors, writing shortly before she died, "I want to spend
my heaven doing good on earth."

All her life she suffered from illness and was always plagued
with fainting spells, yet she worked hard in the laundry and dining
room of the convent. She went without food to gain forgiveness for a
drunkard. Truly a valiant woman, she did not whimper about her
sickness or anxieties. Instead she saw the power of love as a divine
alchemy which can work for the good of all things. The last year of
her life she slowly wasted away of tuberculosis, dying at the age of

only twenty four.

ST. THERESA'S PERSONAL PRAYER

Govern by all thy wisdom, O Lord, so that my soul may always be serving thee as thou dost will, and not as I may choose. Do not punish me, I beseech thee, by granting that which I wish or ask, if it offend thy love, which would always live in me. Let me die to myself, that so I may serve thee: let me live to thee, who in thyself art the true life.

† † † † † † † † †

ST. THIEMO (11th century)   SEPTEMBER 28
Born into Bavarian nobility, he became a monk and gained great fame as an engraver, a painter, and a sculptor.

In 1090, as Archbishop of Salzburg, he was persecuted, imprisoned and exiled for his loyalty to Gregory VII. He joined the crusaders and was captured by the Turks, who imprisoned, tortured, and put him to death.

† † † † † † † † †

ST. THOMAS the Apostle (1st century)   DECEMBER 21
Known as Didymus "the twin," Thomas was selected from among the Galilean fishermen as one of the twelve apostles whom Jesus chose as the foundation of his church. Little is recorded of his life, but his personality seems clear. He was not at all shrewd, but had the spirit of childhood, a simplicity of spirit, following Christ with a string of "whys."

It was Thomas who, when told of the resurrection, said, "Except I shall see in his hands the print of the nails, and put my finger into the place of the nails, and put my hand into his side, I will not believe." And eight days later after Jesus made him place his finger into the wounds, doubting Thomas' incredulity was changed into ardent faith.

St. Thomas is surrounded by several legends which seem to have little relation to the saint, but are most interesting. One says that should one wish to dream of a future husband, peel an onion, wrap it in a handkerchief, and sleep with it under the pillow, invoking St. Thomas before retiring.

Marriages on St. Thomas' feast day, December 21, which is the shortest day of the year, may be blessed or doomed. One version is that one should not get married on that day for to marry on the shortest day of the year is an indication that the marriage will also be brief, for one of the partners will suffer an early death. On the other hand, some say it is a good day for marriage. Again, because it is the shortest day there "will be less time for repentance" and the partners will be less likely to regret their commitment to each other.

To see into the future year, on the evening of December 20, St. Thomas' Eve, throw a shoe backwards over the shoulder, leaving it where it falls without looking at it. The next morning, if the shoe is pointing toward the door, it is a sign that the owner will move during the coming year. If the shoe has landed with the toe pointing inward, there will be no change of dwelling for another twelve months.

PRAYER TO PROTECT CATTLE
Sprinkle the cattle with salt and holy water, and say over each one:
St. Thomas, preserve thee from all sickness.

† † † † † † † † †

ST. URSULA (4th century)   OCTOBER 21
One legendary version of Ursula is that she, the daughter of a Christian king of Great Britain, was asked by the son of a great pagan king to be his wife. Desiring to remain a virgin, she obtained a delay of three years. To serve as companions she was given ten young women of noble birth, and she and each of the ten were accompanied by a thousand virgins. The whole company embarked in eleven ships and sailed the seas for three years. When the appointed time for the wedding had come, and Ursula's fiance was about to claim her, a gale of wind carried the eleven thousand virgins far from the shores of England. They sailed to Cologne where, upon landing, they were massacred by the Huns who were persecuting the Christians.

† † † † † † † † †

ST. VALENTINE (3rd century)   FEBRUARY 14
There are legends of two St. Valentines, both having similar stories.

One was a priest who was arrested for helping Christian prisoners, put in chains, and brought before the court. The judge had a young adopted daughter who had been blind for two years. "If you can restore her sight," he told Valentine, "I will believe in Jesus." Valentine placed his hands upon the eyes of the child and prayed, "Lord Jesus Christ, who are the light of the world, heal your servant." Instantly the child could see again, and the judge and his entire family were converted and baptized. But the emperor was not pleased, and in order to quiet the news about the miracle, the judge's family and Valentine were all killed.

The other Valentine, a Bishop of Terni, reputedly cured the son of the philosopher Crates who was afflicted with an incurable malady. When Abundius, a high ranking government official, heard about the magical cure, he had the miracle worker beheaded.

In medieval days it was believed that the birds chose their mate and began to pair on February 14, and it is for this reason that the day was looked upon as specially consecrated to lovers and as a proper occasion for writing love letters and sending love tokens, whence the origin of sending "valentines."

PRAYER TO FIND A LOVER

Blessed Saint Valentine, I come to you with a heart full of love yearning to share its fullness with another. Help me find this person to share my life which I pledge to fill with understanding, courtesy, fidelity, and temperance. Let the law of kindness rule my life and govern all I say and do. Be with me on my search, Blessed Valentine, and guide my way to one who will care for me as I will care for my life's partner.

† † † † † † † † †

ST. VICTOR (3rd century)   JULY 21

The legend of St. Victor is that when Maximianus Herculius arrived in the district near Marseilles, the Christians were stricken with terror. For Maximianus Herculius was the bloody tyrant who had just massacred the 6,600 members of the Theban Legion. Victor, a soldier in Maximianus' army, took it upon himself to comfort his very frightened co-religionists.

When his efforts were discovered, he was taken to the leader of his unit and told to desist his activities and to remain faithful himself to the gods of Rome. Victor refused, declaring himself "a soldier of

Christ," so he was taken to Maximianus. Here he still proclaimed his faith. Wishing to make an example of him, the emperor ordered him dragged through the public streets and then imprisoned.

Once in prison, Victor converted three other prisoners, Longinus, Alexander, and Felician. When they declared themselves Christian, they were immediately beheaded. Then Victor was beaten, tortured on the rack, and finally crushed under a millstone on the public threshing floor.

† † † † † † † † †

ST. VINCENT de Paul (1576 - 1660)　　　　JULY 19

The third child of a French peasant family, Vincent had three brothers and two sisters. As a youth he tended sheep, and through the sacrifice of his parents, he received a good education and studied at the University of Toulouse.

From birth Vincent seemed to be blessed with a good practical mind, acute discernment, ambition, tenacity, the ability to express ideas clearly, and the faculty of adapting himself to whatever circumstances he encountered. He was a careful man, giving attention to small details and leaving nothing to chance.

After leaving school he had an outstanding career as priest and pastor. His life was devoted to active charity, and no one was excluded. He collected abandoned infants at street corners or on church steps and cared for them. He visited convicts, speaking kindly to them and serving their needs. He ministered to the poor, the blind, fallen women, the infirm, the insane, and the children. His boundless love for the unfortunate made him well-known and respected everywhere.

PRAYER FOR THOSE IN NEED

O glorious Saint Vincent, patron of charitable societies and father of all who are in misery, obtain from thy Lord help for the poor, relief for the infirm, consolation for the afflicted, protection for the abandoned, a spirit of generosity for the rich, conversion for sinners, tranquility and order for all nations, and salvation for all. Let all persons know the effects of thy merciful intercession so that, being helped by thee in this life, we may be united in the life to come, where there will be no grief, sorrow, nor weeping, but joy and gladness and everlasting happiness.

† † † † † † † † †

ST. VINCENT FERRER (1350 - 1419)   APRIL 5

The fourth child of an English father and Spanish mother, Vincent entered the Dominican Order when he was seventeen to become one of the most popular and influential preachers of all time. He also became an adviser to the King of Aragon and Queen Yolanda chose him for her confessor.

One of the greatest orators in history, Vincent converted untold numbers, as many as ten thousand pilgrims following him from one place to another. Every church was filled with both faithful and infidels when he appeared. He preached in Spain, France, Italy, Switzerland, Germany, and Great Britain and he was understood everywhere, even though some say he spoke only in Spanish. Many of his biographers believe that he had the gift of tongues.

His personal life was austere with the floor his usual bed. He arose at two in the morning to pray and celebrate mass. He sometimes preached for as long as three hours, and is credited with hundreds of miracles. After his midday meal, he would tend the sick children, and retire about eight in the evening. He travelled on foot, poorly clad.

PRAYER FOR PARDON AND FAVORS

Glorious apostle and wonder-worker, Saint Vincent Ferrer, receive this humble prayer and send down plentiful showers of divine favors. By the fire of love in thy heart, obtain for us the mercies of pardon and remission of all our sins, steadfastness in faith, and perseverance in good works, so that we may become worthy of thy powerful patronage.

Extend thy protection to our bodies also, and deliver us from sickness. Obtain from God through thine intercession the healing of our spiritual maladies. Let thy heart be tender toward us, O mighty Saint. Stretch forth thy hand over us, and obtain for us those graces for the welfare of both soul and body, which we so earnestly ask of thee.

† † † † † † † † †

ST. VITUS (3rd century)   JUNE 15

According to legend, Vitus—sometimes known as Guy—was a child martyr, son of a pagan senator of Lucania. During the era of the Emperors Diocletian and Maximinian, Vitus' father sought to persuade the boy to renounce his new faith and pay homage to the pagan gods. But Vitus remained steadfast and fled with his tutor Modestus. They went to Rome where Vitus drove a demon out of the son of Diocletian. Yet, because he remained true to his faith, he was tortured to death along with his tutor, Modestus, and his nurse, Crescentia.

† † † † † † † † †

ST. WILGEFORTIS (unknown date)   JULY 20
A fabulous saint known also as Uncumber, Kummernis, Komina, Hulfe, Cumerana, Ontcommene, Dignefortis, Euthropia, Liberate, Reginfledis, Livrade, etc.

The legend is that Wilgefortis, one of nine sisters, was the Christian daughter of a pagan King of Portugal. Her father wanted her to marry the King of Sicily, but she had made a vow of virginity. In order to avoid the marriage she prayed to be disfigured and God caused a beard to grow on her face. The King of Sicily decided he did not want a bearded lady as his wife so he called off the engagement, whereupon her father had her crucified.

† † † † † † † † †

ST. WILLEBRORD (658 - 739)   NOVEMBER 7
A native of Northumberland, England, he went to the monastery when he was six. He was given a good education and trained in missionary work. A handsome, joyous man of wise counsel and pleasant speech, he was energetic in whatever he had to do. Over his almost fifty years of preaching, Willebrord made many converts.

He is invoked for the prevention or cure of convulsions.

† † † † † † † † †

ST. WOLFGANG (934 - 995)   JUNE 7
Born in a German province of a family of counts, he had a religious tutor at home by the time he was seven years old. Later he attended a celebrated monastic school, became a teacher and labored for the reform of the hierarchy of the church.

Though he served as priest, monk, and bishop, his reputation was built on his educational abilities. He was tutor to Emperor Henry

II, who learned from Wolfgang the principles which governed his saintly and energetic life.

Near the end of his life, Wolfgang withdrew from public life, apparently on account of a political dispute, to become a hermit. He was discovered by a hunter and they began the journey back home but, while travelling on the Danube, he fell ill at the village of Pupping. At his request he was carried into the chapel of St. Othmar where he died.

† † † † † † † † †

ST. ZITA (1218 - 1278)   APRIL 27

A naturally happy disposition and the teaching of a virtuous mother caused young Zita to develop a sweet and modest character with a conscientious attention to work. At the age of twelve she entered domestic service in the household of the Fatinelli family and remained there all her life.

She devoted herself energetically to her chores, a quality which did not endear her to the other servants. Her gifts of food to the poor alienated her employers also. However, the ill-will and ill-treatment from both fellow workers and masters was powerless to deprive Zita of her inward tranquility, her love for all people, and her innate generosity. She always believed the best of others, being quick to defend and slow to criticize. As she grew older she was placed in charge of all the affairs of the house, and there were many stories of her good deeds and supernatural manifestations. She died with the same peace and serenity she had always known.

† † † † † † † † †

PRAYERS

Scripture makes clear over and over that a prayer is a direct channel to God. "The prayer of the humble pierceth the clouds" according to Ecclesiasticus 35:17. "Give yourself continually to prayer" says Acts 6:4. "Continue in prayer" is the message from Colossians 4:2. Luke 18:1 admonishes us that "Men ought always to pray, and not to faint." It is also well to note Ecclesiasticus 34:24, "When one prayeth, and another curseth, whose voice will the Lord hear?" Most of all, take heed of Matthew 21:23, "Whatsoever ye shall ask in prayer, believing, ye shall receive."

Prayers must always come from the heart and can be said in one's own words. Sometimes help in formulating one's innermost thoughts is needed, and the devotions in this section can fill that need. There are daily, special occasion, and general prayers as well as specific petitions. Among them you will find one to serve your intention or purpose.

Use these devotions frequently and experience life's deepest satisfaction, for sincere prayer can bring daily nourishment and enrich every encounter with blessings of love and serenity.

THE LORD'S PRAYER (OUR FATHER)
Our Father, who art in heaven,
hallowed be thy name;
thy kingdom come;
thy will be done on earth as it is in heaven.
Give us this day our daily bread,
and forgive us our trespasses,
as we forgive those who trespass against us;
and lead us not into temptations;
but deliver us from evil.

BEFORE A CRUCIFIX
O good and dearest Jesus, before thy face I humbly kneel, and with the most fervent desire of soul, I pray and beseech thee to impress upon my heart lively sentiments of faith, hope, and charity, true sorrow for my sins, and a true desire of amendment, while with deep affection and grief of soul I reflect upon and ponder over Thy five most precious wounds, having before my eyes the words of David, the prophet, "They have pierced my hands and feet, they have numbered all my bones."

HAIL MARY

Hail Mary, full of Grace,
Blessed art Thou amongst women,
and blessed is the fruit of Thy womb Jesus.
Holy Mary, Mother of God,
pray for us sinners,
now and at the hour of our death.

GLORY BE

Glory be to the Father, and to the Son,
and to the Holy Ghost.
As it was in the beginning, is now,
and ever shall be, world without end.

THE APOSTLES' CREED

I believe in God, the Father Almighty, Creator of heaven and earth;
in Jesus Christ, His only Son, our Lord, who was conceived by the
Holy Ghost, born of the Virgin Mary, suffered under Ponitius Pilate,
was crucified, died, and was buried. He descended into hell, the third
day He rose again from the dead, He ascended into heaven, sitteth at
the right hand of God, the Father Almighty; from thence He shall
come to judge the living and the dead, I believe in the Holy Ghost,
the Holy catholic church; the communion of Saints; the forgiveness
of sin, the resurrection of the body; and life everlasting. Amen.

FOR ALL SAINTS

We give thanks to thee, O Lord, for all saints and servants of thine,
who have done justly, loved mercy, and walked humbly with their
God. For all the high and holy ones, who have wrought wonders and
gained great fame, we thank thee. For all the meek and lowly ones,
who have earnestly sought thee in darkness, and held fast their faith
in trial, and done good to all men as they had opportunity, we thank
thee. As they have comforted and upheld our souls, grant us grace to
follow in their steps, and at last to share with them in the inheritance
of the saints in light.

DAILY PRAYERS

SUNDAY   Blessed is this day which has been given. Blessed is
the earth, the heavens and the seas. Blessed are light
and darkness, day and night, birds, beasts, and me.
Let me use this day well. Let me not wander from
thy commandments.

MONDAY	Guide me this day to keep my heart clean, my hands pure, and my mind directed toward the glory of God. Keep my tongue quiet of lies and deceit, and many blessings upon me will surely follow.
TUESDAY	Deal kindly, Lord, with me who lifts up mine eyes to thee. Have mercy on my weaknesses, and grant that my strength will be increased sufficient to the demands made upon me this day. For I know my help is in Thee, who made heaven and earth.
WEDNESDAY	Restore to me the joy of salvation. Strengthen me with a generous spirit. Create a clean heart for me. Renew in me a steadfast spirit. Deliver me from my guilts, and cleanse me from my sins. I know that light shines forth for the just, and joy for the upright of heart.
THURSDAY	Hear my prayer for my heart is faint. Restore me when my faith falters. My foolishness and my faults are known to you. Rescue me from those who hate me. With Thee is the fountain of life, and in Thy light we see light.
FRIDAY	Help me this day to love those who care for me, be kind to those who wish me harm, and to keep my voice gentle, my mind open, and my heart filled with the knowledge that there are many blessings for those who trust in God and keep his commandments.
SATURDAY	Blessed be God who is my shield and my refuge, my fortress and my deliverer. I know that the Lord renders justice to all the oppressed, forgives my faults, and heals all infirmities.

MORNING PRAYER

I come to this new day with a realization that I can make of it a time of growth. Lead me, guide me, and strengthen me as the day unfolds. Help me to see opportunities for good so that my every act and deed will be of benefit to all. Shield me with your protection as I go about my tasks with faith in Thy safe-keeping.

NOONDAY PRAYER

Dear Patron Saint ————, I pause at midday to thank thee for the protection and guidance of the morning hours. Shield me from temptations through the afternoon and evening hours. Be at my side this day and evermore.

EVENING PRAYER

Thou has kept me by your side this day, and I am truly grateful. Forgive whatever mistakes I've made and sins I've committed. Bless me this night with peaceful sleep so that I may serve Thee again tomorrow to the best of my abilities.

A CHILD'S GOSPEL NIGHT PRAYER

Matthew, Mark, Luke and John,
Bless the bed that I lie on.
Before I lay me down to sleep,
I give my soul to Christ to keep.
Four corners to my bed,
Four angels there aspread,
Two to foot and two to head,
And four to carry me when I'm dead.
I go by sea, I go by land;
The Lord made me with His right hand.

BENEDICTION

I pray the prayer many others do,
May the peace of God abide with you,
Wherever you stay, wherever you go,
May the mighty love of God also grow,
Through days of labor and nights of rest,
The love of God will make you blest.

ATTRACT FRIENDS

Help me to be kind and thoughtful in word and deed. Help me to forget myself and draw love and affection from those around me. Increase my force of body and mind to make me inviting to those I find appealing. I am most thankful for the love of others which thou has put into my own heart. Lead me in this search, I ask most humbly.

CONQUER ONE'S FAULTS

My prayer is to conquer pride with humility, wrath with love, anxiety with calmness and confidence, selfishness by generosity, ignorance by learning, evil by doing good, and restlessness with the peace which closeness to God bestows upon me.

DEVELOP DETERMINATION

Awaken my conscious will and energy, for I know there is hidden strength within me to overcome all obstacles and temptations. Do not let my small defeats and discouragements delay me in my determination to succeed in whatever I do. I know that I can overcome failure and disappointment, and with thy help, become a stronger, sturdier, and more disciplined person.

FOR DETACHMENT

Great Saint –––––, obtain for me the grace of never attaching my heart to the fleeting goods of this life. My vanity and my greed serves nothing which will enrich my spiritual life, and I need thy help in keeping my sights set on the uplifting spiritual values of caring only for others. My needs will be met in the same measure with which I share with those whose needs are more urgent than my own.

FOR GUIDANCE

Lord God, king of heaven and earth,
this day, direct, rule and govern
my mind, my heart, body, thoughts, words, and deeds
so that now and forever more
I may experience salvation and true freedom.
O Savior of the world, help me.

FOR GUIDANCE

I ask thee, Blessed Saint –––––, for thy blessing and thy guidance as I face the tasks of life. Help me to always aim high in my ambitions and to enlarge my vision of the possibilities for growth, for love, and for service to others. Show me each day how to make my good intentions turn into benefits for those I encounter. Let my light shine always with a kindly glow.

FOR THE HOME

Almighty God, and Glorious Saint –––––, we commend to thy continual care our home and all that dwell therein. Fill each one of us with faith, virtue, temperance, patience, love, and affection. Grant each the strength and courage for the battle of life. We ask these things in humble gratitude for the blessings already bestowed upon us.

FOR JUSTICE

Almighty God and Glorious Saint —————, I beseech thy advocacy on my behalf. Give to those who judge the spirit of wisdom and understanding that they may discern the truth. Allow them to render justice moderated with compassion and mercy.

FOR A PEACFUL DEATH

O Jesus, and Blessed Saint —————, you have known the anguish of my heart, the bitter agony of my spirit, and the suffering of my body. Help me in this hour. Though I walk through the shadow of death, I will fear no evil, for Thou art with me. I have comfort and consolation by Thy presence and Blessed Saint —————, hold my hand. Take my sins, which are many, and let thy grace sustain me. Lead me through my sorrow to the ultimate faith that I shall enter into joy everlasting.

FOR RECOVERY OF HEALTH

Merciful God, I appeal to Thee and to you, Glorious Saint —————. I beg humbly and from my heart, take me into thy care. Fold me in your arms, and ward off my fears, soothe my pains, and guard me against the despair which threatens my spirit. Show me the path I need to take to effect a return to well being. Comfort me in my affliction, succor me in my distress, remain with me, strengthen me, and bless me with a return to health.

FOR RELEASE FROM OBSTINACY

O Blessed Saint —————, deliver me from futile hopes and struggles against insurmountable odds. Let me realize that faith in one's ability to conquer obstacles should remain firm, but give me the humility to acknowledge that there are objectives which are beyond my reach. Do not let me cling to impossible dreams instead of turning to productive work toward achieving small successes which will bring everwidening horizons to my life.

FOR A SPECIAL FAVOR

Blessed Saint —————, grant me thy help. I have need of this special favor and I call upon you for assistance. My request is for ————— (state favor desired). It is with faith in thy powers I ask thee, and with confidence in thy mercy and generosity toward my request.

FOR THE SICK

O God, and Glorious Saint —————, look down from heaven and

grant thy servant the help of thy power that, according to thy good pleasure, the sickness may be turned into health, and the sorrow into joy. Look down in mercy, bestow thy comfort, and instill sure confidence in thy healing hands.

FOR SPIRITUAL BLESSINGS

Holy God, and Glorious Saint —————, I come to ask thy blessing for my empty heart and tired soul. I am enmeshed in the world, its ways, its habits, its vanities. Help me to become less interested in material things, and more concerned in the search for the peace of mind and joy which comes with true faith in the goodness of God. Grant me the grace to be zealous in this resolution to turn my will and my life over to His care. I pray for the strength and ability to pursue the path of godliness, with the assurance that my new heart and my revived spirit will be filled with the magnificent gifts which come to all who love God fully.

FOR VITALITY

Dear God, and Saint —————, help me to form good habits which will protect both my mind and body from the darkness of sickness. Let me exercise sensibly and eat only wholesome foods so that I do not cause myself suffering. Charge my soul with joy, my mind with power, and my body with vitality so that I may serve Thee well.

FOR WISDOM

God, grant me the serenity
to accept the things I cannot change,
The courage to change the things I can,
And the wisdom to know the difference.

GRATITUDE FOR HEALTH

I come to thank Thee, O Lord, for the blessing of good health which has been given unto me. I awake each morning with a grateful heart for my body is without pain, my mind is clear, my spirit is tranquil, and my soul is filled with love of life and of You. Keep me ever close with Thy care.

GRATITUDE FOR RESTORED HEALTH

O God, and Blessed Saint —————,
I now appear before thy most holy face,
and thank thee from my innermost soul,
because thou hast raised me from my sickbed.

My plea was heard and I was given the strength
to overcome my affliction. Thy mercy has brought
me to my feet and better health.
Help me to use my recovery for good, for in my
sickness I have learned that worldly goods have
the value of dust. Let me use my recovery as a
gift from God, and share my gratitude with love
for others and assistance to anyone who needs my caring.

IN PRAISE OF BLESSINGS

When I doubt myself, remind me of my successes.
When I falter, strengthen me with the knowledge
that I have come this far with Your help.
When I am sorrowful, bring me only a day of
sunshine, a child's laughter, a single
flower bud, or the sound of a simple song.
Teach me not only to be grateful, but to
share my blessings with others who may
not have so many as I.

OVERCOME ANGER

Teach me to be only angry with anger and with nothing else. Help me to reject the poison of rage for it kills a peaceful heart. Let me calm the wrath of others by the good example of my tranquility, and soothe resentment and irritation with torrents of love.

OVERCOME FEAR AND WORRY

Blessed Saint ————— I ask for your blessing that I may eliminate from my life anxiety and fears. The past is gone and cannot be changed, tomorrow is not yet here and should not claim my attentions. It is to this day only I am responsible. With God, around me, protecting me, I will banish the gloom of fear which darkens my way and leads me to stumble into error.

SETTLE A DISTURBED HOME

Holy Father, I beg of Thee, and Glorious Saint ————— to bless my home. Let it become a fortress manned by love, and kindness, and consideration between all who live here. Take from us the manners that irritate, the words which aggravate, and the bitterness which may reveal itself in our attitude. Visit this place with your gentle presence so that we may evermore be knit together in peace and with love.

WHEN IN PAIN

Most merciful God, and Blessed Saint —————, allow this pain I bear to serve as a reminder of the greater suffering you have borne. Enfold me with thy love for I know the hurt will subside in time, but your light will shine on me always. Mercifully accept this prayer, and grant thy servant the help of thy power.

TO ALL SAINTS FOR MANY BLESSINGS

Give me thy blessings as I face the tasks of life. Show me the way toward all that is good, and warn me when I stray from the path you would have me trod. Guide my feet toward your kingdom, place in my hands the work you would have them do, and instill in my mouth only those words which are kind toward those to whom and of whom I speak. Keep my mind clear and clean with thoughts which are acceptable and pleasing to you.

TO A GUARDIAN ANGEL

My guardian angel, Blessed Saint ————— (insert name)
I honor and love you as my special friend.
Be with me at my side to guard me and care for me,
and to guide me as I go about my life this day.

ST. APPOLONIUS' PRAYER FOR FAITH

O Lord Jesus Christ, give us such a measure of thy Spirit that we may be enabled to obey thy teaching: To pacify anger, to take part in pity, to moderate desire, to increase love, to put away sorrow, to cast away vain-glory; not to be vindictive, not to fear death; ever entrusting our spirit to immortal God, who with thee and the Holy Ghost liveth and reigneth world without end.

ST. GELASIAN'S PRAYER FOR PEACE

O God, who art Peace everlasting,
whose chosen reward is the gift of peace,
and who hast taught us that the peacemakers are Thy children,
pour Thy sweet peace into our souls,
that everything discordant may utterly vanish,
and all that makes for peace be sweet to us forever.

ST. IGNATIUS LOYOLA'S PRAYER

Teach us, good Lord, to serve Thee as Thou deservest:
To give and not to count the cost;
To fight and not to heed the wounds;

To toil and not to seek for rest;
To labour and not ask for any reward
Save that of knowing that we do Thy will.

TO INFANT OF PRAGUE FOR GUIDANCE AND WISDOM
I come to you with thanksgiving. You have fortified me on every side by providing for my needs. Speak to me now and help me to understand what you want of me. Fill my conversation with wisdom, and my silence with holy thoughts. Guide me with the Holy Spirit that I may bless you always for what you have done.

TO OUR LADY OF FATIMA FOR HUMILITY
AND SPIRITUAL RICHES
Blessed be thy name. Protect me from vanity and deceit, for I know it is only in humility that I can hope for security. I know that in building my spiritual house, your blessing will be upon me today and always. Let me be an instrument in bringing joy to others for that is surely the way my soul will be made joyous.

TO SAINT CYRIL FOR DAILY NEEDS
Let thy blessing rest upon us, we pray. We praise thee for all thy good and perfect gifts. We know thy loving kindness will bestow upon us all things we truly need, and you will surely provide all those requirements for which we are most grateful.

TO SAINT ELENA TO OVERCOME DISTRESS
May this burden of grief, sorrow, and suffering be lifted from my aching heart. Replace these afflictions with the healing love which will lift me out of my despair. Banish bitterness from my mind and turn my sad thoughts toward happy memories, gratitude for the good which remains in my life, and the serenity with which to go forward to a truly happier future.

TO SAINT RAYMOND FOR A BLESSED HOME
In the name of the Holy Father, Blessed Mary, and their son Jesus, I beseech thy blessing to enter my home. As each one here is touched with thy love, may it spread and multiply a hundredfold. Grant each of us the grace to live peacefully, unselfishly, and with courtesy toward one another. Let the light of understanding and love shine bright forevermore.

TO SACRED HEART OF JESUS FOR DAILY BLESSINGS

Grant me clarity of mind, a healthy body, and a peaceful soul so that I may go about my daily work with composure, tranquility, and efficiency. Keep me this day in Thy eye for in Thee I put my trust.

TO ANY SAINT FOR ASSISTANCE

O Saint of God, Blessed Saint ————— (name)
Who is placed at His right hand,
Thy prayers be like a rampart
As against the foe we stand.
Pray for us, Saint —————,
and help me in this plea.
———————— (state purpose)
I give this situation to you humbly
and with confidence in the knowledge
that, with your prayers and intercession
in this matter, justice, goodness, and
mercy will prevail.

Portrait of St. Francis, Said to Date from 1225

HEALTH CONDITIONS

To alleviate, cure, help, improve, prevent, or protect from:

CONDITION	PATRON SAINT
Acne	Rock
Alcoholism	Matthias
All patients	Camillus de Lellis
All physical disease	Rock
All sickness - physical, mental, or spitirual	Raphael
Anxiety	Wilgefortis
Any physical disease	Rock
Apoplexy	Wolfgang
Arthritis	Maurice
Blindness	Genevieve - Odilia - Raphael - Valentine
Blood disorders	Agatha
Breast diseases	Agatha
Cancer	Giles - Rita
Childbirth	Leonard
Children's intestinal diseases	Erasmus
Chorea (St. Vitus' dance)	Vitus
Colds	Erasmus
Colic	Erasmus
Contagious diseases	Rock
Contagious fevers	Christopher
Convulsions	Willebrord
Coughs	Blaise - Quentin
Cramps	Maurice
Crippling diseases	Giles
Delirium	Giles
Depression	Job
Diarrhea	Lucy
Dog bites	Hubert
Dry skin	George
Dying patients	John of God
Dysentery	Lucy
Eczema	George
Epidemic infections	Rock
Epilepsy	Balthasar - Valentine - Vitus - Willebrord

91

CONDITION   PATRON SAINT

Expectant mothers ....Margaret
Eye Disease........................... Clare - Cyriacus - Lucy

Fainting spells.................................... Valentine
Fever....................... Benedict - Genevieve - Gertrude

Goiters .... Blaise
Gout .... Maurice

Hardening of the arteries.......................... Wolfgang
Headache........................... Acacius - Dionysius
Healing of the sick............. Michael the Archangel - Raphael
Hemorrages........................Agatha - Lucy
Hemorrhoids.................................Fiacre
Hernia.. Gomer

Incurable diseases .... Valentine
Infections .... Christopher
Inflammation of the joints .... Maurice
Inflammatory diseases............................Benedict
Insanity....................................Dympna - Giles
Insomnia................................... Seven Sleepers
Invalids .... Rock
Itch .... George

Kidney diseases................................Benedict
Knee troubles .... Rock

Lameness...................................... Rock
Leg Problems.................................. Servatus
Loss of leg....................................Giles
Loss of sight ....Odilia
Lumbago..................................... Lawrence
Lymph gland diseases ....Balbina

Madness.................................Giles - Hubert
Mental retardation............................. George
Metabolic diseases............................. Maurice
Miscarriages.......................... Catherine of Sweden

HEALTH CONDITIONS - Continued

CONDITION	PATRON SAINT
Nervous disorders	Dympna - Vitus
Nightmares	Giles
Obsession with demons	Dympna
Pains of childbirth	Erasmus
Panic	Giles
Paralysis	Pantaleon - Wolfgang
Plague	Christopher - Francis Xavier - Rock - Valentine
Poison	Benedict - Martin of Tours
Possession by spirits	Cyriacus - Raphael
Pregnancy	Margaret
Rabies	Hubert - Vitus
Rheumatism	Lawrence
Sick children	Clement
Sickness of any kind	Rock - Vitus
Skin diseases	Anthony - Benedict - George - Rock
Sleeping sickness	Vitus
Small pox	Matthias
Snake bites	Paul - Vitus
Sore throat	Blaise
Sores	George
Spiritual and bodily health	Mary, Blessed Virgin
Sterility in women	Giles
Stomach diseases	Erasmus
Sudden death	Andrew Avellino - Christopher
Syphilis	Job
Throat diseases	Blaise - Suitbert
Thyroid gland diseases	Blaise
Toothache	Apollonia - Blaise - Christopher
Tuberculosis	Pantaleon
Tumors	Fiacre
Ulcers	Job
Violent Death	Barbara
Whooping cough	Blaise

St. Augustine at Prayer

PATRON SAINTS
of Businesses, Groups, Jobs, Professions, Trades

Actors . . . . Vitus
Alcoholics . . . . Matthias
All who work with hammers . . . . Eligius
All workers . . . . Joseph
American Blacks . . . . Martin de Porres
Animals . . . . .Anthony
Any dangerous work . . . . .Barbara
Archers . . . . Christopher
Architects . . . . Blaise - Louis
Art . . . . Catherine of Bologna
Artillerymen . . . . .Barbara
Artists . . . . .Luke
Astronomy students . . . . .Albert
Aviators . . . . Theresa of Lisieux

Bailiffs . . . . .Ives
Bakers . . . . .Nicholas
Bankers . . . . .Matthew
Barbers . . . . .Cosmas & Damian - Louis
Beasts of Burden . . . . Blaise
Beauticians . . . . Louis
Bees . . . . .Ambrose
Beggars . . . . .Giles
Bell Ringers . . . . .Barbara
Biology students . . . . .Albert
Blacks . . . . Peter Claver
Blacksmiths . . . . Eligius - Giles
Boatmen . . . . .Clement - Julian - Nicholas
Bookbinders . . . . Barthalomew
Bootblacks . . . . Nicholas
Box Makers . . . . .Fiacre
Boy Scouts . . . . George
Brewers . . . . .Augustine - Nicholas
Bricklayers . . . . Vincent Ferrer
Builders . . . . Blaise - Louis
Burglars . . . . .Nicholas
Bus Drivers . . . . Christopher
Butchers . . . . Barthalomew

Cab Drivers . . . . Eligius
Cabinetmakers. . . . . Anne - Victor
Candle Makers and Sellers . . . . .Ambrose
Captives. . . . . Leonard - Nicholas
Carpenters. . . . . .Anne - Joseph - Matthias - Wolfgang
Carvers . . . . Blaise
Charitable societies . . . . Vincent de Paul
Chefs. . . . . .Barbara - Lawrence
Chemistry students . . . . .Albert
Children's Nurses. . . . . .Concordia
Choirboys . . . . .Holy Innocents
Circus People. . . . . .Julian
Clock Makers. . . . . Eligius
Cloth Makers. . . . . Maurice
Clowns . . . . .Genesius
Coal Miners. . . . . Leonard
Cobblers . . . . .Crispin & Crispinian
Comedians. . . . . Genesius - Vitus
Concrete Workers . . . . Vincent Ferrer
Condemned Prisoners . . . . .Quentin - Zita
Conscientious Objectors . . . . Martin of Tours
Cooks . . . . Barbara - Lawrence - Zita
Coppersmiths . . . . Leonard
Cow Herders . . . . Gomer
Cripples. . . . . .Giles

Dancers . . . . .Francis de Sales - Vitus
Dangerous jobs of any kind. . . . . .Barbara
Distillers . . . . Louis
Dock Workers . . . . Nicholas
Doctors. . . . . Cosmas & Damian - Pantaleon - Raphael
Dogs . . . . Hubert - Vitus
Domestic Animals. . . . . .Ambrose
Domestic Workers. . . . . Martha - Zita
Druggists. . . . . Cosmas & Damian
Dyers. . . . . Maurice
Dying Patients. . . . . .John of God

Educators of young girls . . . . .Ursula
Embroiderers. . . . . .Clare

Engaged Couples . . . . Valentine
Engravers. . . . . .Theimo
Evangelists. . . . . .John the Baptist
Exorcists . . . . .Cyriacus
Experimental Sciences students. . . . . .Albert

Farm Workers . . . . Eligius
Farmers. . . . . Eligius
Feeble people . . . . Camillus de Lellis
Ferrymen . . . . .Julian
Firefighters . . . . .Eustace
Fireworks Makers . . . . .Barbara
Fish Dealers. . . . . Andrew the Apostle
Fishermen .Andrew the Apostle - Nicholas
Foresters. . . . . Hubert
Foundry Workers . . . . .Barbara
Fruit Dealers . . . . Christopher
Furriers. . . . . .Simon

Gamblers. . . . . Camillus de Lellis
Gardners . . . . .Adam - Fiacre
Gilders. . . . . .Clare
Glass Dealers and Makers. . . . . .Luke
Glove Makers. . . . . Mary Magdalene
Goldsmiths . . . . Eligius
Green Grocers . . . . Leonard
Gunners. . . . . .Barbara

Hair Dressers . . . . Louis
Hired Hands . . . . Notburga
Horses . . . . Anthony of Padua
Hospitals .Camillus de Lellis - John of God
Hotel Keepers . . . . Martha
Housekeepers . . . . Anne - Notburga - Zita
Housewives . . . . Anne
Hunters . . . . Hubert

Impossible Cases . . . . .Jude
Impoverished People . . . . .Giles
Infantry Soldiers . . . . Maurice

Innkeepers. . . . . .Julian - Martha
Intellectuals. . . . . .Catherine of Alexandria

Jockeys. . . . . Eligius
Journalists. . . . . Francis de Sales
Judges. . . . . Catherine of Alexandria - Ives

Knife Grinders. . . . . .Catherine of Alexandria

Laborers . . . . Eligius
Lacemakers. . . . . .Luke
Lathe Operators .Catherine of Alexandria
Laundresses. . . . . .Clare
Lawyers. . . . . Catherine of Alexandria - Ives
Leather Merchants. . . . . .Crispin & Crispinian - Peter - Simon
Leather Workers . . . . .Crispin & Crispinian
Librarians . . . . .Jerome
Locksmiths . . . . .Eligius - Leonard - Peter
Lovers . . . . Anthony of Padua - Raphael - Valentine
Lunatics . . . . Dympna

Maids. . . . . Zita
Male Children . . . . Felicitas
Manual Laborers . . . . Felicitas
Marriages. . . . . Anthony of Padua
Mentally Retarded Persons . . . . George
Merchants . . . . .Francis of Assisi - Nicholas
Metalworkers. . . . . Eligius
Midwives. . . . . Cosmas & Damian - Raymond Nonnatus
Military Engineers. . . . . .Barbara
Millers. . . . . .Catherine of Alexandria
Mineralogy students . . . . .Albert
Miners. . . . . .Barbara - Eligius - Leonard
Missionaries. . . . . .Francis Xavier - Theresa of Lisieux
Motherhood . . . . Gerard Majella
Mothers. . . . . Anne
Motorists. . . . . Christopher
Mountain Climbers . . . . Bernard
Mules. . . . . Anthony of Padua
Music. . . . . Cecilia

Musical Instrument Makers . . . . Cecilia
Musicians. . . . . Cecilia

Natural Science students . . . . .Albert
Navigators . . . . Erasmus
Needleworkers. . . . . .Clare
Notaries. . . . . .Mark
Nurses . . . . Agatha - John of God - Raphael
Nursing Mothers . . . . .Concordia

Old Maids . . . . .Andrew the Apostle - Catherine of Alexandria
Orators . . . . .Catherine of Alexandria
Organ Builders. . . . . Cecilia
Orphans. . . . . .Holy Innocents

Painters . . . . Catherine of Bologna
Patients . . . . .Camillus de Lellis
Pawnbrokers . . . . .Nicholas
Perfumers . . . . Mary Magdalene
Pewter Makers. . . . . .Fiacre
Philosophers . . . . .Catherine of Alexandria
Phrenology students . . . . .Albert
Physicians . . . . .Luke
Physiology students. . . . . .Albert
Pilgrims. . . . . Nicholas
Plasterers. . . . . Barthalomew
Plastics Manufacturers. . . . . .Barbara
Playing Card Makers . . . . Balthasar
Plumbers. . . . . Vincent Ferrer
Poets. . . . . Cecilia - Nicholas
Poor People. . Anthony of Padua - Francis of Assisi - Vincent de Paul
Porters. . . . . Christopher
Precision Instrument Makers . . . . Hubert
Printers . . . . .Augustine
Prisoners . . . . Hubert - Leonard - Nicholas
Prostitutes. . . . . Mary Magdalene
Public Speakers . . . . .Catherine of Alexandria

Repentant Girls and Women . . . . Mary Magdalene
Restaurant Owners . . . . Lawrence

Robbers. . . . . Nicholas
Rope Makers . . . . Catherine of Alexandria - Paul

Saddle Makers . . . . Crispin & Crispinian - Catherine of Alexandria
Sailors . . . . Erasmus - George - Nicholas
Scholars. . . . . Catherine of Alexandria
School Children. . . . . Holy Innocents - Nicholas
School Girls. . . . . .Ursula
Scientists. . . . . .Albert
Sea Travellers . . . . .Gertrude
Seamstresses . . . . Anne
Servants. . . . . .Notburga - Zita
Shepherds . . . . .Cuthbert
Shoe Makers . . . . Crispin & Crispinian - Peter
Shoe Repairmen . . . . .Peter
Shop Keepers . . . . Nicholas
Sick Animals or People . . . . .John of God
Singers. . . . . Cecilia
Sinners . . . . .Peter
Slaves . . . . Peter Claver
Smelters . . . . Stephen
Social Workers. . . . . Frances of Rome
Soldiers. . . . . George - Joan of Arc
Song Writers . . . . Cecilia
Spinners . . . . .Catherine of Alexandria
Stablemen. . . . . Anne
Stevedores. . . . . .Nicholas
Street Pavers . . . . Rock
Stonecutters . . . . Stephen
Stonemasons. . . . . Blaise - Stephen
Students . . . . Albert - Catherine of Alexandria - Jerome
Surgeons . . . . Cosmas & Damian - Luke - Rock

Tailors. . . . . Gerard Majella - Matthias
Tanners. . . . . Bartholomew - Catherine of Alexandria
Tax Collectors. . . . . .Matthew
Taxi Drivers. . . . . Eligius
Teachers . . . . Catherine of Alexandria - Jean Baptiste
Television . . . . .Clare
Theologians. . . . . .Augustine

Those in need . . . . Giles
Those obsessed by the devil. . . . . Dympna
Those unhappily married. . . . . Gomer
Those who care for the sick. . . . . Camillus de Lellis
Those who serve the poor and needy. . . . . Martha
Those who wish to marry . . . . Valentine
Tilemakers. . . . . Fiacre - Rock - Vincent Ferrer
Tool Makers . . . . Eligius
Trappers . . . . Hubert
Travelers . . . . Christopher - Nicholas - Raphael
Truck Drivers . . . . Christopher

Unmarried men . . . . Andrew the Apostle - Luke
Unmarried women. Catherine of Alexandria
Used clothing dealers. . . . . Anne - Rock

Veterinarians. . . . . Anthony - Eligius
Virgins. . . . . Catherine of Alexandria

Weavers . . . . Blaise - Crispin & Crispinian
Wheel Makers . . . . Catherine of Alexandria
Wheelwrights. . . . . Catherine of Alexandria
Widows . . . . Felicitas
Wild Animals. . . . . Blaise
Wine Makers . . . . Vincent Ferrer
Women . . . . Anne
Wood Cutters . . . . Gomer
Working Women . . . . Martha
Writers. . . . . Francis de Sales

Young Girls. . . . . Irene
Young and innocent people. . . . . Raphael
Young men . . . . Aloysius Gonzaga
Youth . . . . Aloysius Gonzaga

Zoology students. . . . . Albert

He keepeth the paths of judgment, and preserveth the way of his saints.

Proverbs 2:8

SPECIAL PURPOSES
Various objectives, pleas, protections, situations

Against earthquakes . . . . Francis Borgia
Against evil forces. . . . . Thomas
Against fire . . . . .Agatha - Barbara - Lawrence
Against hail. . . . . .Christopher - Paul
Against impenitence at death . . . . Christopher
Against impure thoughts. . . . . Martin of Tours
Against insanity. . . . . .Dympna
Against mice . . . . .Servatus
Against miscarriages . . . . Catherine of Sweden
Against perjury . . . . .Felix
Against poverty. . . . . Anne
Against racial injustice. . . . . .Martin de Porres
Against rats. .Martin de Porres - Servatus
Against rats and mice . . . . .Gertrude
Against robbers. . . . . .Nicholas
Against snakes. . . . . Patrick
Against storms. . . . . Christopher - Erasmus - Scholastica
Against sudden death . . . . .Andrew Avellino - Christopher
Against temptations of the devil .Benedict
Against terrors of the night. . . . . .Giles
Against thunderstorms . . . . .Barbara
Against wild beasts . . . . Blaise
Against witches. . . . . Thomas
Assist in bearing daily trials with patience. . . . . .Mary Magdalene
Assistance for the poor . . . . .Holy Rosary
Avoid gossip . . . . Catherine of Sweden
Avoid sin. . . . . .Mary, Blessed Virgin

Become generous. Faith, Hope & Charity
Bring justice . . . . .Ives - Louis
Bring rain . . . . Odo

Calm children . . . . Dionysius
Calm those possessed. . . . . .Genevieve
Cause virtue to flourish . . . . .Holy Rosary
Communicate with spirits . . . . .Genevieve
Conquer every temptation. . . . . .Lucy
Conquer fear. . . . . George
Control animals. . . . . Gerard Majella

SPECIAL PURPOSES - Continued

Control one's tongue............................ Louis
Control the temper .... John the Apostle
Cure cattle diseases............................ Thomas
Cure sick animals.............................. Blaise
Cure sick horses............................... Eligius

Defeat the devil........................... Dionysius
Deliver the possessed.............. Cosmas & Damian - Cyriacus
Deliver souls from purgatory..................... Holy Rosary
Deliverance from enemies......................... Michael
Destroy vice .... Holy Rosary
Detect evil plots .... Frances
Dream of a future husband .... Lucy

Ease childbirth .... Erasmus
Encourage good humor...................... Teresa of Avila
Endure suffering............................... Job
Exorcise demons........................ Anthony the Great
Express thoughts and ideas clearly .... Vincent de Paul

Family unity................................. Joseph
Find a husband .... Valentine
Find lost articles .... Anne - Anthony of Padua
Find a wife .... Valentine
For acceptance .... Paul
For all mankind.............................. Clement
For all needs .... Joseph
For an alcoholic .... Matthias
For assistance .... Martin de Porres
For a blessed home .... Raymond
For blessings .... Anne
For blessings of humility..................... Bernadette
For compassion.......................... Pantaleon
For courage................................. George
For daily blessings..................... Sacred Heart of Jesus
For daily needs .... Cyril
For a desperate situation...................... Jude - Rita
For fertility............................ John the Baptist
For fidelity to chosen vocation .... Frances
For gift of speaking......................... Augustine

For God's love. . . . . Barnard
For good crops . . . . Gertrude - John the Baptist
For a good death. . . . . .Ursula
For good luck . . . . .John the Baptist
For good weather . . . . .Clare
For guidance and wisdom . . . . Infant of Prague
For healing . . . . Bernadette
For health. . . . . .Mary, Blessed Virgin
For healthy babies. . . . . Raymond Nonnatus
For a holy death . . . . .Andrew Avellino - Joseph - Paul
For a holy life. . . . . .Bede
For humility . . . . Catherine of Bologna - George
For humility and spirituality. . . . . Teresa of Avila
For interracial harmony .Martin de Porres
For justice. . . . . .Basil
For lost articles . . . . Anthony of Padua
For many blessings . . . . All Saints
For men who have troublesome wives. . . . . Gomer
For a miracle. . . . . .Anthony the Great
For necessities. . . . . Martha
For pardon and favors. . . . . Vincent Ferrer
For patience . . . . Mary Magdalene
For protection. . . . . .Barbara
For purity . . . . Joseph
For seekers of faith . . . . Benedict - John the Apostle
For seekers of wisdom. . . . . .Augustine
For self-improvement . . . . Mary Magdalene
For special requests. . . . . Anthony of Padua
For spiritual growth . . . . .Holy Rosary
For spiritual healing . . . . Anne
For spiritual riches . . . . Our Lady of Fatima
For strength . . . . Augustine - Peter
For tranquility . . . . Anne
For understanding. . . . . .Clare
For women who have unfaithful husbands . . . . .Frances
Foretell the future. . . . . .Frances
Forgiveness for drunkenness . . . . Theresa of Lisieux
Forgiveness of sins. . . . . .Peter

Gain spiritual strength. . . . . .Mary, Blessed Virgin

SPECIAL PURPOSES - Continued

Get a husband . . . . Catherine of Alexandria

Have all angels intercede in behalf of request . . . . Holy Rosary
Have dream of a future husband . . . . Lucy - Thomas
Have sins forgiven . . . . Holy Rosary
Have special protection . . . . Holy Rosary
Heal animals . . . . Blaise - Rock
Help in all difficulties . . . . Anne - Joseph
Help in times of despair . . . . Faith, Hope & Charity
Help with study . . . . Albert - Bede

Improve the memory . . . . Anthony of Padua
Improve work habits . . . . Ambrose
In an emergency . . . . Expeditus
In desperate situations . . . . Jude - Rita
In lawsuits . . . . Agia
In time of need . . . . Raphael
Increase one's faith . . . . Faith, Hope & Charity

Love all persons . . . . Francis of Assisi - Theresa of Lisieux

Make peace . . . . Isabel
Mercy for criminals . . . . Quentin

Never be defeated by misfortune . . . . Holy Rosary

Obtain all that is asked for . . . . Holy Rosary
Obtain good lodging while travelling . . . . Gertrude
Overcome addiction to alcohol . . . . Matthias
Overcome addiction to gambling . . . . Camillus de Lellis
Overcome misfortunes . . . . Eustace
Overcome panic . . . . Giles
Overcome pride . . . . Holy Rosary
Overcome the sin of excesses . . . . Jerome
Overcome temptations . . . . Jerome

Predict the future . . . . Thomas
Protect against evils of soul and body . . . . Clare
Protect against fire . . . . Eustace
Protect against fires of eternity . . . . Eustace
Protect dogs . . . . Vitus

SPECIAL PURPOSES - Continued

Protect from accidents .... Christopher
Protect from burglars .... Nicholas
Protect from evil................................... Michael
Protect from impure thoughts and actions .... Louis
Protect from liars .... Felix
Protect from volcano eruptions...................... Agatha
Protect from virgins................................. Irene
Protection in times of epidemics...................... Rock
Protection when needed .... Patrick

Quiet noisy people .... Cyriacus

Read consciences............................... Genevieve
Read minds.................................. Gerard Majella
Receive special graces .... Holy Rosary
Resist impure thoughts .... Agatha
Resist temptation to sin .... Michael the Archangel
Restore faith............................ Theresa of Lisieux
Restore peace .... Cyriacus

Safe childbirth................................... Leonard
See the future .... Columba - Genevieve
See over far distances .... Gerard Majella
Settle arguments.................................. Isabel
Settle disputes.................................. Expeditus
Slay dragons of the heart.......................... George
Solace for those condemned to death .... Cosmas & Damian
Speak only kind words .... Catherine of Sweden
Special favors .... Anne - Bernard
Spiritual and bodily health .... Mary, Blessed Virgin
Strength to cope with physical handicaps .... Bede
Strengthen one's faith.............................. Basil
Success in any endeavor .... Servatus
Sustain hope when depressed .... Faith, Hope & Charity

To be more caring of others .... Mary Magdalene
Triumph over misfortune .... Holy Rosary

Victory in battle .... Michael

SPECIAL PURPOSES - Continued

When afraid............................Andrew the Apostle
When bored...............................Francis of Assisi
When discouraged ....Barnabas
When falsely accused.....................Raymond Nonnatus
When in need.............Mary, Blessed Virgin - Vincent de Paul
When a lawsuit has been lost........................Nicholas
When unjustly accused ....Nicholas
Withstand the cold ....Cuthbert
Women who wish to have children ....Andrew the Apostle

St. Bonaventura shows St. Thomas the Crucifixion

QUOTATIONS OF THE SAINTS

The world is a great book, of which they who never stir from home read only a page.

St. Augustine

It is better to keep silence and to be, than to talk and not to be. It is a fine thing to teach, if the speaker practices what he preaches. Now there is only one teacher who spoke and it came to pass, and the things which he did in silence are worthy of the Father. He that truly possesses the word of Jesus is able also to listen to his silence. Nothing is hidden from the Lord, but our own secrets are near him. Let us therefore do everything, knowing that he dwells in us, so that we may be his temples and he himself be in us as our God.

St. Ignatius

Let us learn upon earth, those things which can prepare us for heaven.

St. Jerome

Sorrow is given us on purpose to cure us of sin.

St. John Chrysostom

All blessings come to us through our Lord. He will teach us, for in beholding his life we find that he is our best example. What more do we desire from such a good friend at our side? Unlike our friends in the world, he will never abandon us when we are troubled or distressed. Blessed is the one who truly loves him and always keeps him near.

St. Teresa of Avila

No one will tell a tale of scandal, except to him who loves to hear it. Learn then, to check and rebuke the detracting tongue, by showing that you do not listen to it but with displeasure.

St. Jerome

Beware of despairing about yourself: you are commanded to put your trust in God, and not in yourself.

St. Augustine

The true measure of loving God is to love him without measure.

St. Bernard

QUOTATIONS OF THE SAINTS (Continued)

Love, indeed, is the source of all good things; it is an impregnable defense, and the way that leads to heaven. He who walks in love can neither go astray nor be afraid; love guides him, protects him, and brings him to his journey's end.

St. Fulgentius

It is no great thing to be humble when you are brought low; but to be humble when you are praised is a great and rare attainment.

St. Bernard of Clairvaux

Be always employed about some rational thing, that the devil find thee not idle.

St. Jerome

Let us faithfully transmit to posterity the example of virtue which we have received from our forefathers.

St. Peter Damian

When the truth shines out in the soul, and the soul sees itself in the truth, there is nothing brighter than the light or more impressive than that testimony. And when the splendour of this beauty fills the entire heart, it naturally becomes visible, just as a lamp under a bowl or a light in darkness are not there to be hidden. Shining out like rays upon the body, it makes it a mirror of itself so that its beauty appears in a man's every action, his speech, his looks, his movements and his smile.

St. Bernard

Nothing is so strong as gentleness: nothing so gentle as real strength.

St. Francis de Sales

Three things are necessary for the salvation of man: to know what he ought to believe; to know what he ought to desire; and to know what he ought to do.

St. Thomas Aquinas

It is in vain to gather virtues without humility; for the spirit of God delights to dwell in the hearts of the humble.

St. Esasmus

QUOTATIONS OF THE SAINTS (Continued)

Let us faithfully transmit to posterity the example of virtue which we have received from our forefathers.

St. Peter Damian

Where your pleasure is, there your treasure: where your treasure, there your heart: where your heart, there your happiness.

St. Augustine

God hath promised pardon to him that repenteth, but he hath not promised repentance to him that sinneth.

St. Anselm

Misfortune is never mournful to the soul that accepts it; for such do always see that in every cloud is an angel's face.

St. Jerome

When you say your prayers, you must go into your private room, and shut the door, and say your prayers to your Father who is in secret. And your Father, who sees what is done in secret, will give you your reward in full. For, when the door is shut, someone prays in his private room when, while his mouth is silent, he pours forth the affection of his heart in the sight of the heavenly pity. And the voice is heard in secret, when it cries out in silence with the holy desires.

St. Gregory the Great

It is a fearful mistake to believe that because our wishes are not accomplished they can do no harm.

St. Gertrude

Regret not that which is past; and trust not to thine own righteousness.

St. Anthony

This is the very perfection of man, to find out his own imperfection.

St. Augustine

What is faith unless it is to believe what you do not see?

St. Augustine

We shall steer safely through every storm, so long as our heart is right, our intention fervent, our courage steadfast, and our trust fixed on God. If at times we are somewhat stunned by the tempest, never fear. Let us take breath, and go on afresh.

St. Francis de Sales

God has been very gracious to me, for I never dwell upon anything wrong which a person has done, so as to remember it afterwards. If I do remember it, I always see some other virtue in that person.

St. Teresa of Avila

Do not look forward to what may happen tomorrow; the same everlasting Father who cares for you today will take care of you tomorrow, and every day.

St. Francis de Sales

Habit, if not resisted, soon becomes necessity.

St. Augustine

INTERNATIONAL IMPORTS
PUBLISHER & DISTRIBUTOR OF NEW AGE BOOKS

BOOKS IN PRINT